# Praise for *Brand*

"The VERY first thing any business should how to let clients sell themselves on your brand before they even call you. HIGHLY recommend reading these golden nuggets." —**Joe Crisara, America's Service Sales Coach**

---

"In business, sometimes you don't know what you don't know. We assumed that we had a recognizable identity because customers often mentioned our truck wraps, but man—we were wrong! It wasn't until we started working with Dan that we came to truly understand the power of a cohesive brand. Dan's vision helped us align all our visual elements, clearly communicate our premium service offerings, and lay the foundation for our growth. I highly recommend acting on everything Dan recommends in this book!" —**Tommy Mello, President, A1 Garage Door Service; Author,** Home Service Millionaire; **and Host, "Home Service Expert" Podcast**

---

"Long before I met him, I saw the great work Dan and his company did on branding and rebranding by 'KickCharging' it with a great-looking truck design. I was so impressed that my franchise hired him for a redesign of our logo and brand. And now so many of my consulting clients have experienced the same phenomenal results too. This book is sharing so much. There's no fluff. It's written in an easy way to read and for you to follow along. There are so many great examples that help illuminate the difficult ideas that ONLY Dan could make clear by removing the clutter just like his rebrands and redesigns do. Read it. Underline it. Take action on it!" —**Al Levi, Author and President, 7-Power Contractor**

---

"Dan is truly a master of his craft. As someone who's seen the before and after of KickCharge's work firsthand, glimpsing into the mind that has rejuvenated so many home service companies is a game changer. If you run a home service business, you owe it to yourself to buy this book." —**Ryan Redding, CEO, DP Marketing Services**

---

"After years of single-digit growth, I knew we needed to make a radical change in our branding. Everything Dan did for us is outlined in the road map he presents in this book. His recipe for branding has helped us grow from $2.2 million to $12 million in 36 months." —**Jason Buehler, CEO, Buehler Air**

---

"My single biggest takeaway having gone through the rebranding process with Dan is don't be complacent. I don't think I fully understood how the new brand not only affected our external marketing, but our internal marketing as well. This book lays out the blueprint for how a home service company needs to brand themselves to attract the best customer and the best employees, and spend less on marketing in the process. Since rebranding 3 years ago, we've grown from $5 million a year to pacing $25 million in 2022." **—Victor Rancour, CEO, Absolute Airflow**

"A common stereotype is 'I can't afford a rebrand.' What people don't understand is that they simply cannot afford NOT to rebrand. There is no greater return on investment than branding with Dan and the KickCharge team. It'll change your life, just like it changed mine. This book lays out the plan on how to build a brand that not only consumers love, but employees love, too." **—Amanda Triolo, CEO, Grasshopper Heating & Cooling**

"Dan Antonelli is a genius when it comes to creating a brand for home service businesses. He has created brands for many of my clients helping them create a powerful, market-disrupting identity for their business. Branded Not Blanded is a must read for any home service business that wants to go from being unnoticed in their community to being a recognized community icon. Dan IS 'The Brand Man!'" **—Richard Behney, Owner, Million Dollar Plumber Coaching; and Host, "Potty Talk" Podcast**

"Buyer beware! If you enjoy spending a ton of money on marketing efforts that do not produce results, tirelessly trying to explain your value to clients who see you as 'just another company,' and blending in with every other home service business in your market, this book is not for you. Dan is THE AUTHORITY on branding in the home service space. This book is a must-read for anyone who is looking to maximize their marketing dollars, expand their presence, and gain attention for all the right reasons in their respective market. Working with Dan and his team has not only been a wonderful experience, but offered REAL results that we can quantify." **—Texas Medley, President and CEO, Medley Heating and Air Conditioning**

*"Very few walk their talk quite as well as Dan Antonelli and his team at KickCharge. They are THE AUTHORITY and most referred company when it comes to rebranding, logo design, vehicle wraps, and creative marketing strategies in the home service space. Whether you're just starting your business or searching for a way to get a leg up in your market, this book is for you! In this book, Dan gives you a peek behind the curtain as to what he and his team do for clients around the world and delivers a step-by-step process you need to go through to truly separate your business from the competition and avoid overpaying on advertising to get your phone to ring."* **— Evan Hoffman, Co-Owner, On Purpose Media, and Co-Host, "HVAC Success Secrets Revealed" Podcast**

---

*"We know how a brand affects companies' ability to market effectively. If you need to get your 'brand voice' right before you add the megaphone, this book will be invaluable. A quality brand decreases your marketing costs and allows word of mouth to spread; that's why I've been joyfully spreading the good word about Dan Antonelli and KickCharge™ and why I will share this book far and wide!"* **—Tim Brown, Founder, Hook Agency**

---

*"It was only five minutes into our first call before Dan verbalized the future of our company. 'Timo'—it's friendly; it's inviting. I'm picturing a smiling serviceman on the side of the van, six feet tall. Something kids will point to when they see it.' I asked, 'Are you sure? I want to look like a big company.' Dan replied, 'Do you want to look like a big company or become a big company?' Dan went on to create one of the most recognizable mascots of the entire home service industry. Our logo was featured on the cover of* SignCraft Magazine, HVACR Business Magazine, *and* Signs of the Times. *I'm forever indebted to Dan and for the brand he nurtured over the past decade. With his help, we grew to become the largest HVAC company in our service area and ultimately exited after being acquired by a private equity firm for a locally record-breaking multiple. Crossing his path was nothing short of life-changing, as is the knowledge he shares in this book. Don't pretend to be a big company; become one."* **—Joey Timo, President, Timo's Air Conditioning & Heating**

---

# BRANDED NØT BLANDED

## KICKCHARGE™ YOUR HOME SERVICE BRAND

# Dedication

One doesn't get to write a book like this without being blessed with the help of so many other people along the way. To the business owners who have trusted me and the team at KickCharge™, I can't thank you enough for giving us the opportunity and trusting us to build your brand and help change your lives. Waking up each day and getting to see how our work has impacted you is what motivates me today and has for over 25 years.

To my teammates at KickCharge™, thank you for believing in our mission and for always designing like lives are at stake. I am incredibly blessed to have such an amazingly talented group of brand designers, illustrators, wrap designers, writers, and account managers who share my vision. Without you, none of this happens.

To my wife, thank you for your support of my passion and for all you do to support our family. Without you, none of this works. To my beautiful girls, continue to strive for excellence in everything you do.

And to the doctors who gave me the gift of life after my double bypass surgery last year, I am blessed beyond belief to still be here today and continue to be grateful every day.

# Acknowledgments

To the design community who always support me and my mission, I am so grateful for your support.

To my dear friend Burt Arthur, thanks for giving me a job working in your sign shop 35 years ago. That was my first exposure to working with small businesses and the trades. The knowledge you passed on to me is visible in nearly every job we do.

To my amazing editor and proofreader Loretta Mowat, thank you for helping to make this book the best it could be. I couldn't have done it without you.

# TABLE OF CONTENTS

# FOREWORD

## Ken Goodrich on Branding Goettl

# A boy and his flashlight.

It was 30 degrees in the desert that night. My dad said, "Go get the flashlight; I need your help." I was 10 years old and my dad needed help fixing a neighbor's furnace.

I still remember how proud I was walking up to the door to let the homeowners know we were there. I felt like Batman & Robin were coming to save the day! When the door opened, my dad said, "Hi, Chuck. We're here to fix your furnace!" (It's kind of like saving the day, just a bit less dramatic.) As I walked toward the furnace, I pushed the red flash button on the flashlight and lit up the furnace. It was glorious!

Do you know why they call it a "flashlight"? Because back when flashlights were invented, the batteries didn't last long, so one would have to flash short beams of light to see their way and conserve the battery. Anyway, the light shined on the furnace and displayed the coolest logo I had ever seen. It was like a smashed diamond, with a blue background, silver letters, and a red stripe. It was cool. The word inside the logo was weird. I certainly couldn't say it. The word was GOETTL, and when I asked my dad how to say that word, he gruffed, "Figure it out."

As time went on, I worked with my dad holding the flashlight, carrying the tools, cleaning things—you know the drill. My dad became a Goettl dealer, and I spent most of my formative years installing and repairing Goettl air conditioners side-by-side with him. Those were some of the best years of my life.

Forty-two years since the first night I held the flashlight for my dad, I was presented with the opportunity to buy Goettl. I had come full circle. Back to the place where it all began. Back to the future. I was so excited I said, "I'll take it!" and the broker said, "Don't get too hasty; take a look at the books first." Goettl was what the Wall Street guys call "out of favor" or "underperforming" or what I call "broken." On top of cultural, legal, and reputational challenges, Goettl was bleeding cash. My lawyer said, "Better stay away from this one," and my wife agreed. So did my accountant, my industry friends, my personal friends, and anyone else I shared the opportunity with. In fact, every person I discussed acquiring Goettl with gave me a thumbs-down. Yet I couldn't let it go. It was my destiny.

The business was struggling, yet I had a hunch. My hunch was that the silver, blue, and red Goettl badge that caught my eye forty-two years ago was the gem inside that business. And if I could find the expertise that could help me tap into that 80-year-old brand equity and marry that with the boy with the flashlight story, that would be the catalyst for the resurrection of Goettl. So, I started googling, and I ran across this book called *Building a Big Small Business Brand: How to Turn Your Brand into Your Most Valuable Asset* by Dan Antonelli.

I ordered the book immediately and read it cover to cover. In the book, Dan talked about how the logo serves as the foundation

for the brand. How the logo should convey expertise, creating an expectation of quality displayed in a nostalgic manner and conjuring feelings of times when quality and service trumped catchy slogans or promises of low prices. Once I looked at his work, I knew Dan was the man to build the Goettl brand!

Isn't it great when you find someone passionate about the work they do, and you get to be the customer? I know it doesn't happen that often, yet that's the way it was from the very beginning working with Dan. He was excited, he had a vision, and he led me toward the pursuit of perfection. In our first interaction, I said, "I want a logo and brand foundation that portrays the feelings of this one radio ad created by Roy H. Williams for Goettl."

It went like this: "I was a 10-year-old boy holding the flashlight for my dad while he worked on an air conditioner for a customer. His name was Duncan Goodrich. He didn't talk much, but there's a certain kind of magic that happens when a boy holds the flashlight for his father. I held it steady and quiet, and Dad talked to me while he worked.

# At Dad's funeral, I realized that every time he handed me that flashlight, he was passing the torch.

"He said, 'When a person needs help, you go right away, not when it's convenient for you.' He said, 'Always do the right thing. Always do what is right.' And he said, 'The Goettl iron horse is a magnificent machine; nothing else even comes close.' That was the first time I held the flashlight for my dad but it wouldn't be the last. At Dad's funeral, I realized that every time he handed me that flashlight, he was passing the torch. And my dad believed in Goettl air conditioners, so I bought the company. Goettl. G-O-E-T-T-L: It'll keep you cool, but it's hard to spell. Now we'll respond right away and do the right thing always. No one knows air conditioning like Goettl.'"

And he nailed it. The boy with the flashlight coupled with the iconic Goettl badge depicted in a nostalgic manner reinforced the two converging stories, giving the viewer a feeling of confidence in the brand while reinforcing the heart of the brand.

Once the logo was complete, the truck wraps were installed, and the radio ads began to play, the phones never stopped ringing. I have never experienced anything like it! Customers called in to say, "I don't need your service right now, but I can't wait until my air conditioner breaks so I can call you!"

Customers were astonished that the logo matched the story, which gave them confidence in the brand. Our technicians reported: "Our customers are so happy to see us!"

And to drive the brand story deep into the hearts and minds of our customers, Dan created the innovation of our team gifting a Goettl vintage flashlight on every job. To date, our team has gifted over one million flashlights throughout the southwestern United States.

So, my hunch was right. The true heart of Goettl was its brand. Despite the advice from experienced counsel to run, I followed my heart and found a way to shout the Goettl story from the mountaintops!

## So, my hunch was right. The true heart of Goettl was its brand.

Since the rebrand, Goettl has grown more than 20x its acquired revenue, opened eight additional locations, grown to over 1,000 team members, and commanded the highest valuation to date of any company in its sector. The brand told the story, the story connected with the customer, and the customer connected with the team.

As I reflect on this journey, and more specifically the resurrection of a brand, I'll leave you with these thoughts. Your brand is the heart of your company. It's the story that tells people who you are. The story that connects them to you and makes them like and trust you before you ever do business. It's the secret sauce, your secret weapon, your leg up, so choose your brand architect wisely. Thanks, Dan, and Team KickCharge™ for giving new life to this iconic brand—the right way, not the easy way.

**—Ken Goodrich, CEO,**
**Goettl Air Conditioning & Plumbing**

INTRODUCTION

# BUILD A BRAND— NOT A BLAND

# Listen up. The truth may hurt.

If you're reading this book, you may be the owner of a home service business or an employee of one. Perhaps you want to rebrand the business. Prepare yourself; some of what I'm about to say may make you uncomfortable. You may question what you're doing with your current brand. I might even piss you off because you suddenly realize you haven't leveraged your brand properly.

But here's the good news. You're here now. You're thinking about not being complacent, and you know what you are doing today is not good enough for tomorrow. And chances are, your competitors aren't thinking like that at all. There is a high likelihood their brands do in fact, for lack of a better word, suck. Which is terrific for us. Therefore, I ask you to be open to the concepts we cover here.

And if you're about to launch a new business, then this book is going to save you a ton of headaches later and, hopefully, a ton of money too. Because you're going to learn how to do this right from the start.

On a personal note, I am a champion of small businesses. I especially love helping the underdogs. I hope this book helps them compete with the bigger companies asleep at the wheel. The surprising thing about most of the bigger companies is that the bigger they get, the more complacent they become. This is your opportunity to leverage their complacency and gain some market share!

## Living the dream.

Thirty-seven years ago, at the tender age of 15, I hand-painted and lettered my first home service truck. It was for a chimney sweep company based in Staten Island, NY, where I grew up. I had always been fascinated with lettering and, later on, logo design. At 17, I was blessed to get hired to work in a sign company, working under a great sign artist named Burt Arthur, where we created signs and truck lettering for many small businesses, including a lot of home service businesses.

I was blessed to be taught so much about the fundamentals of design, especially on vehicles. To this day, that knowledge and experience has served me well. You really can't replicate the experience of hand-lettering a truck by sitting in front of a computer screen. It's just not the same.

I loved working with entrepreneurs, and even at that age, I realized what a special opportunity it was to help create things that would help their businesses to prosper—in essence, to help change their lives. Imagine how cool that is, to realize at such a young age what it was you were passionate about. Imagine finding your "why" before you're even 18.

I wanted to become a full-time sign painter upon graduating from high school, but my parents thought it would be better for me to go to college. So I attended the University of Scranton, earning a degree in Communications, with a focus on Advertising. I continued

*I guess you could say I was destined to work with home service contractors. Here's me at age 18 hand-lettering a plumbing company truck in 1988.*

painting signs and doing truck lettering throughout college while learning the fundamentals of graphic design along the way.

I graduated from college and got a job as a designer in New York City. I worked there for five years, rose through the ranks, and was doing well. But I missed working with entrepreneurs. Creating brochures for a health insurance company was somewhat soulless work. I wasn't affecting any meaningful change, and I sure as hell wasn't changing lives.

So I started my sign and design business on the side while working full-time, which is something I'm sure most of the entrepreneurs reading this book can relate to. Then, for six months or so, I hustled as I had never hustled before, trying to build my design business focused on small businesses. After months of 100-hour weeks, I had enough work to quit my day job and pursue my dreams full time.

Twelve years after lettering that first home service truck, I was back at it doing what I loved. And here I am today, 27 years later, still living the dream and changing lives daily. I've had the pleasure and privilege of working with over 2,000 entrepreneurs since starting my agency. We've helped them grow their businesses, create jobs, and make meaningful changes in their businesses. For me, it doesn't get any better than that. I especially love when I'm speaking at various trade shows and I get to meet some of these entrepreneurs we've worked with, and they're so grateful for what we helped them to build—I don't think I can ask for a better reward.

## Building on *Building a Big Small Business Brand.*

It was almost 10 years ago that I wrote my book *Building a Big Small Business Brand*. In it, I laid the foundation for why branding is so important to small businesses. Since then, our work has become more and more focused on home service businesses, and probably 90% of our work is now dedicated to the branding and marketing of home service businesses.

Within this book, I summarize over 25 years of branding experience for you, so you can better understand how to leverage your brand with success.

So what has changed in the last decade? I think the core philosophy remains the same, but we've homed in more on the idea of disruption and on building brands that stand out and don't fit in.

That is the most important aspect of home service branding: standing out, not "blanding." Most home service companies don't have a brand at all. Maybe they have a logo, but it's likely not even a good logo, and whatever they do have blends in with what everyone else has. **And because they have neither a compelling brand nor a brand story to accompany it, they spend more money than they need to market their business.**

**Read that part again.**

# The weaker your brand, the more money you will spend to market your company.

So while it may suck to realize your home service brand is not working, that realization brings great opportunity. You can change the direction of your company and be more effective in your marketing spend. You will also improve your culture and your ability to recruit.

The beauty of branding, and not blanding, is based on *opportunity*.

**The opportunity to:**

  • **Leverage your competitors' weaknesses.**

  • **Build a better culture.**

  • **Make your marketing work harder.**

There are so many weak brands in the home service space that it's easy to leverage their complacency. *All you have to do is build a better brand.*

And that's what I love about what we do. We assist our clients to take market share from complacent companies with weak brands, or "blands." And we do it with a smaller marketing budget than the competitors use for their entire marketing and advertising spend.

## The industry is changing.

Recent times have brought so much more private equity into the marketplace, which has made branding even more important. For those private equity firms looking to acquire home service businesses, it's more than just a multiple of earnings before interest, taxes, depreciation, and amortization (EBITDA). They are looking more closely at how a brand performs in a market. What is the company's reputation? Is there consistency in how the company is marketed? Are all their channels speaking with the same voice?

We've seen several of our clients sell their businesses to private equity, earning much higher multiples than ever before. It's been exciting to see how much they were able to get for their business. It's also rewarding to hear how much their brand factored into the final sale price, which further reinforced the enormous return on

*Timo's, one of the first home service brands we rebranded in 2012, was recently sold to private equity.*

their branding investment. Hansen Heating and Air is just one of the many examples that show how branding can help change the trajectory of a home service business with sound management and organizational skills. They originally came to us with four trucks on the road in 2013 and sold the business in 2021 for over $50 million.

But while there is significantly more emphasis on branding, there are still a ton of just plain awful brands out there. And that includes some of the larger private equity-owned companies. It also includes many privately owned companies that continue to believe their current success justifies staying the course with their weak, ineffective brands. I see their weaknesses as an area for a better-branded company to come in and make their marketing work harder, perform better, and take more of their market share, all while doing it with less money. I only see opportunities with the current state of branding in the home service industry.

Recently we have focused much more on using data to support our initial theories on brand disruption. We now have almost two decade's worth of experience and have branded thousands of businesses. While we still love to design beautiful brands for our clients, we love to see the results of our work even more.

It's more than knowing the brands are working; it's assessing how marketing spends are being utilized and the results attained before and after rebranding. And I think that knowledge and experience has proven time and again that building a unique and disruptive brand that delivers a positive brand promise is something every home service business should do.

In addition to gathering data, we've also assessed consumer behavior as it relates to purchasing decisions for home service:

- **How does branding affect perceptions?**

- **How does it help companies get higher average tickets?**

Much of our thought process for building brands goes back to figuring out how to build compelling brands that appeal to homeowners.

## Complacency is abundant.

My goal is to help educate home service owners on how important the brand is to achieving success. I am going to share what I've learned from 30 years of building brands for home service businesses. As I mentioned earlier, there is no shortage of really awful branding. And when I see it, honestly, I'm sad, and I'm also disappointed in whoever sold that branding to the owner in the first place. In some instances, perhaps it's the owners themselves who are responsible for the branding. But if it's a third party who gave bad advice or sold them a design with little chance for it to be effective, it makes me upset. So many missed opportunities and wasted resources.

# The fastest-growing and most successful companies we have worked with are run by people who are not complacent.

If you accept the premise that nothing you are today is good enough for tomorrow and imagine the possibilities of what a great brand can do for your business, I think you'll learn a lot. The fastest-growing and most successful companies we have worked with are run by people who are not complacent. They understood that everything they had done so far was not good enough to take them where they wanted to go.

## Designing like lives are at stake.

Imagine you are tasked with creating a brand to help grow your business. You better know what you are doing. You better treat it as a sacred responsibility and design it as if lives are at stake. Far too often, the people giving advice or doing the actual designing are wholly unqualified to do so. Experience matters, as does results.

Beware of who you take advice from. At KickCharge™ Creative, we've had the unfortunate experience of needing to rebrand dozens of companies given bad advice from "marketing coaches" and similar types of self-proclaimed "gurus" whose only supposed branding qualification was their experience in growing their own service business. So let me state unequivocally: that type of experience, while admirable, doesn't make you an expert on branding. What does make you an expert is decades of experience perfecting and honing your craft, studying results, and understanding the role branding plays in your marketing channels.

I'm blessed to be able to participate in many Facebook groups for home service owners. The experience has been enlightening. I see such a profound misunderstanding about the role brands play in building a successful business. And I'm saddened, at times, to see some of the advice given to owners and how that poor advice can really hurt those businesses. Whether it's misinformation about consumer psychology or lack of understanding about logos in general, the end result is often an owner who loses the opportunity to better their business with a better brand strategy.

If I can help an owner understand more about the role branding plays and help them become a student of the craft, they will know how to leverage a better brand themselves. They'll be a more educated consumer in choosing the right design agency to partner with on this endeavor. And they'll be better able to discern a good brand from a poor one and use that knowledge to assess where they stand currently. Clearly, based on the sheer number of poor brands out there, there are a good number of owners who simply don't know any better. This is understandable because it's not their job to know. Just like it's not my job to know how to do a load calculation for my home.

The quantity of skilled designers and agencies who understand branding for small businesses, and specifically home service, is rather small. It's not your web design company. It's highly unlikely to be your sign or wrap company. It's usually not a marketing consultant. Even a graphic designer is largely unqualified to do branding. And it's highly unlikely to be the crowdsourced designer from overseas. Remember, graphic design and branding, while related, are different skill sets. The same can be said about many self-proclaimed marketing gurus, who may be skilled in executing marketing plans but lack expertise in branding home service businesses.

# My goal is to help educate home service owners on how important the brand is to achieving success.

Skilled logo and brand designers are extremely rare. To give you an example, we recently hired a brand designer and received over 200 applications from graphic designers. Out of the 200, only two were qualified at the level we'd expect for our standards. That's one out of 100 designers, essentially.

The crowdsource space is full of people who claim to be qualified brand designers. But most of them are doing a great bit of harm to the home service businesses that hire them. If I can help an owner understand more about brands and how to effectively build one, they'll be more likely to build a brand that can power their business forward and maximize their investment. And while the crowdsourcing space seems like an economical way to brand your company, it's not, because the most expensive logo you'll ever buy is the one you paid the least for. (Read that part again!)

Of course, branding alone won't make your business successful. Even the best branding can't save a company that doesn't have the proper processes and leadership team in place. You will see the highest returns when you combine great branding with great leadership and a well-run business.

There are plenty of books on branding, but not many specifically written for home service businesses. My last book was written with small business owners in mind. This book focuses on all the aspects of building a brand for home service companies. They may share some commonalities with retail-centric small businesses, but home service companies have unique branding needs.

# CHAPTER 1

# BRAND BASICS

# Branding means opportunity.

Branding has become so much a part of the vernacular for home service brands. From my perspective, it's great to see more company owners pay attention to the importance of branding their business.

It's also very rewarding to see how branding has affected the valuations of some of the companies we've branded. One of our clients recently sold their business for the highest multiple ever recorded for a home service brand, and that helps validate the importance of the investment.

A more significant emphasis has been placed on truck wraps in the last decade, which, dollar for dollar, remains the least expensive advertising for home service businesses. With that emphasis comes more owners trying to make sure their wraps are designed well, and they take full advantage of the opportunity an effective brand can have on their marketing.

But there are still many home service companies that have never embraced the value a solid brand brings to their business. Often, it's due to a lack of understanding. You sometimes hear the common refrain "You don't know what you don't know," which certainly can apply to the fundamentals of branding.

I think that sometimes the chatter about branding can feel overwhelming or not relevant to most contractors. Much of what's been written before has tackled branding from a much larger corporate perspective. So before we get into the nitty-gritty behind the premise of this book, we do need to start with the basics of what branding means for home service companies and how it's relevant to their success. Some of what I'll share here about the basics was already presented in my last book, *Building a Big Small Business Brand*. But it's important to repeat some information, especially for those who haven't read that book.

## Branding is like a wheel.

Lots of people think their logo is their brand. It's not. But it is the foundation to help craft your brand. After years of thinking about branding, I haven't come up with a better way to illustrate what a brand is than the wheel analogy. If you imagine your brand as

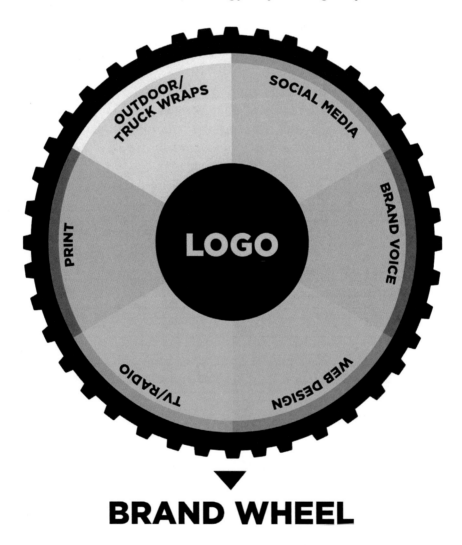

**BRAND WHEEL**

a wheel, at the center of that wheel is your hub. The hub is your logo. The spokes around that wheel represent all your marketing channels that help tell your brand story and build your image.

Just like you can't build a wheel without a perfectly round hub, the same analogy applies to your branding. Getting that hub perfect is critical; otherwise, your wheel will never turn properly. Likewise, neither will your marketing.

When the hub is not round, you can still technically build a wheel. And with enough effort, you can turn that wheel. It will move forward with the right amount of energy. That energy is your marketing spend. And with the right amount of money, sure, it will spin. The perfect wheel will have the hub solid, as well as the spokes that comprise the various touchpoints that your customers will interact with.

But wouldn't it be easier to just try and spin a wheel that's round instead of a misshapen one? Most home service businesses never build a wheel. And when the marketing keeps failing to deliver the return on investment (ROI) they hope for, many simply believe the answer lies in spending more money on their marketing—instead of stopping to fix the root cause of the problem.

One of the most puzzling things about purveyors of marketing and advertising services to contractors is why they don't address brand deficiencies before taking your money. Why don't they advise you of the limited success they may have with your marketing spend because your brand foundation is so poor? To put it another way, why would you ever put a supercharger in a car with four flat tires? Sure, it will move the car, just not very fast or efficiently. Yet so many of these companies will happily take your money.

It may not be a very smart business strategy for us, but we say no quite often to potential clients with poor brands who won't change their branding. Why? Well, because we know it's not going to work correctly. And quite honestly, I'm not comfortable taking money for work I can't stand behind.

But I digress. Let's get back to that wheel analogy. The most efficient wheel is a perfectly rounded one. Misshapen and out-ofbalance wheels, of course, do turn. But the idea is to get all the spokes on that wheel in perfect alignment and harmony. That's why it's important to examine branding in its totality, not just how well your truck wrap and your website work. How do all these pieces function together in delivering your brand story and brand promise to the people you are trying to reach?

Outside of the hub (logo) perhaps not being solid, we often see this brand wheel too heavily supporting a singular aspect of a brand, while other areas around the wheel are ignored and not properly attended to. For example, if you look at your marketing mix and nearly all your resources are put there, you're missing out on the area touchpoints that also serve an important role in establishing your brand in the marketplace.

The basic point here is that brand consistency matters a lot. Think of it this way: When all aspects of your brand work in harmony, that wheel is going to spin with the least amount of resistance. And the least amount of resistance translates into the least amount of money spent on marketing, which of course means increased profitability.

**You can think about brands in this manner:**

- **A brand is what people feel about your company and perceive it to be.**

- **A brand is what people say about you behind your back (your reputation).**

- **A brand is how people would describe your company to their friends and neighbors.**

The key to understanding branding is to always remember that it's not what you say your company is or is not—it's what your customers say it is!

The beauty of today's technology is that you have so many additional sources of information to help demonstrate to you what people are saying about your company. Whether that commentary is lurking on community Facebook pages or in the reviews you are getting (which isn't the same as talking behind your back but still is helpful), you are hearing things about your brand from those sources.

So how do you try and control that narrative? That's the million-dollar question. **How do we get the customers to feel something about your business—especially the ones who have never used your services?** Consistency in what you present to those homeowners is certainly a huge part of helping to form a positive impression—which goes back to the same reason why the logo is such a critical component.

Of course, after you perform services for that homeowner, they will solidify their impression of your company and brand. That's why the service performed after that doorbell is rung or that first phone call is received by that homeowner is so important.

## Touchpoints of your brand.

The most critical thing to remember about the brand wheel is that every single element should be consistent in its presentation. By doing this, you create a brand experience that is more likely to be remembered. This is why colors, fonts, layout, and design elements in your brand should be religiously maintained.

It may seem trivial if the fonts for your new billboard are changed or there is a new color added to your color palette. But these details are important to the continuity of your brand message. Think about bigger companies whose brands you know. As soon as you see an ad, you know the company. That's the same theory we're working toward for your home service as you build a brand. So just be cognizant of the work you contract out, and ensure that your brand standards are maintained no matter what.

Here are some of the touchpoints (or spokes) of the brand wheel with which to coordinate those brand impressions:

- **Stationery**
- **Social media**
- **Print ads**
- **Truck wraps**
- **Interior space and wraps**
- **Uniforms**
- **Radio**
- **Outdoor**
- **Voice**
- **Brochures/collateral**

# Apex Plumbing embraces the power of the brand wheel.

These images illustrate the integration of many of the components of the brand wheel discussed earlier. In March 2021, **Apex Plumbing** launched their new start-up the right way—by investing in a great brand and then integrating it across their channels. From March 2021 through April 2022, **they generated $7.45 million in revenue.**

We love it when we have the opportunity to produce all the elements of that brand wheel for our clients. Why? Because we know that every single thing we produce for that client will 100% be on brand. But sometimes after we've designed the brand and truck wrap for our clients, they may take the logo and go "rogue" on us, so to speak. By that I mean they've given the artwork to another marketing company, sign company, T-shirt screen printer, or web company. And then, sadly, we start to see a degradation of the brand we just worked so hard to create.

Often the first sign of degradation of a brand is when a client needs additional truck wraps designed, and their vendor is unable to follow the brand guidelines well enough for a different truck. How that brand translates from one canvas to another is critical, especially since your vehicles will deliver the most impressions to your potential customers compared to any other medium. Whether a homeowner sees your company's pickup or your van, they should immediately be able to identify it as your brand.

## Brand story and branding.

The idea behind the brand story revolves around your "why" and how it is communicated to your customers (and, of course, why they should care about it). There are several good books about how businesses can find their "why" and how to build brand stories around it.

The primary objective of a brand story is to help explain what you do, how you do it, and why you do it. It should illustrate and represent your company's mission, vision, and values. And the basis of that story should help build trust and loyalty with your brand.

We want the brand story to help cut through the clutter of meaningless advertising homeowners receive. We want them to feel something about your company and connect on some meaningful level while encouraging them with a call to action. We want you to be remarkable in the eyes of the people we believe to be your key audience. And of course, we want them to remember you.

If we consider who we are targeting, bear in mind that the messaging needs to speak to the homeowners. The story should help communicate the following:

- **I know what you do and why you do it.**

- **I connect to the messages you put out there because they're relevant to me on some level.**

- **I feel something about your company because the messages that I've heard were engaging enough for me to have them register (create empathy).**

- **I would like to engage with the company because I connect with them and share their values.**

They've never taken the time to explain their "why," and all their advertising is generally based on vague bullshit puffery that nearly all consumers see right through—and as such, it's completely ignored. Bottom line, they have messaging, if you can even call it that, but no one cares about it.

# The vast majority of home service businesses have no real brand story at all.

Look at most ads for HVAC. What are they almost always all about? Pricing. Oh, wow, I can get a rebate up to $2,000 on a new 16 SEER energy-efficient furnace. Wow, whoopty freakin' doo.

Even some of the largest HVAC companies in the country would be hard-pressed to describe their brand story and what it is. Vague notions of "fast service," lame "guarantees," and "honesty" buzzwords litter their messages. But at the end of the day, no one really cares about their advertising, because it's no different than anyone else's. You could simply swap the logo off one company's ad and replace it with another's, and none of it would make any difference to the consumer. Because no one cares about it.

Contrast that with the brand storytelling Goettl Air Conditioning & Plumbing used to promote their brand: a boy holding the flashlight for his dad while he fixed an air conditioner. That kernel of an idea laid the foundation for one of the most successful and largest HVAC brands in the country. People connected with the "why," which was so beautifully told through print and radio. They understood that Goettl represented an experience, and their voice was authentic.

The ads created that connection and empathy to distinguish them from every competitor in their space, and propelled them from $7 million to $200 million in revenue in eight years. And they did it while providing premium service, with some of the highest ticket averages in the industry. They somehow managed to do the impossible. They got people to feel good about paying for a premium experience. Later on, they expanded on their story to also speak about this amazing brand promise wrapped in a nice tagline: "We do things the right way, not the easy way." Not only does that speak to homeowners, but it also lays the foundation for establishing how the internal culture of Goettl is meant to perform. It is a brand story element that speaks to both external and internal audiences very well, which is very difficult to do.

How much market share do you suppose they took from their competitors and their weak branding? Do you think anyone would suggest that the investment in branding wasn't well spent? That's the difference with a visionary like Ken Goodrich, who took over Goettl, which was, at the time, foundering and losing money. Ken understood why building that perfect brand wheel and brand story was critical to achieving the lofty growth goals he established.

**The reason why so many home service businesses hit a wall with their growth and higher ticket prices is because they offer no legitimate reason for a homeowner to feel good about paying for their service.** They haven't been able to establish empathy; they haven't communicated their "why" appropriately, and therefore, people don't see the value in the prices they're trying to get. Even with the best sales coaching in the world, it's difficult to overcome price objections when the homeowner can't perceive value.

I saw this recently when I spoke with a $40 million home service company about rebranding. Their existing brand was relatively weak and amateurish, but they were growing and doing well. Their ad spend, at 10%, was more than I'd generally like to see. I asked them what their brand story was. They literally couldn't tell me anything unique or interesting or that presented a valid reason that would mean anything significant to the market they served. Vague notions about guarantees, highly trained and trusted professionals, and showing up on time—yawn. They just said everything that everyone says.

Here's an easy test to discern whether or not you legitimately have the foundation of a unique brand story infused in your marketing.

## Zero to hero overnight!

"I decided to rebrand because what we had before wasn't a brand. It was just a clip art logo like everyone else had. I'm in a competitive market with hundreds of companies and I wanted to stand out and be different. My biggest surprise after rebranding was how quickly it went to work for us. We went from zero to hero overnight. You look good, you feel good, you play good. Our brand has attracted new players to the team, grade A talent that we have never had before. Our closing ratios and average tickets are up after rebranding. People feel more comfortable spending their hard-earned dollars with us. Revenue before rebranding was $400,000 (first year of COVID, worst year ever). First year after rebrand, $1.5 million. Second year on track for $2.5 million." —*Frankie Mason, Breckinridge Heating & Cooling, Louisville, KY*

Simply go to your website, and every time you see your company name, replace it with the name of your biggest competitor. Then reread your site. Does it still make sense? If the words on your site aren't unique to you, then neither is your brand story.

Therefore, as a consumer, you offer nothing unique to me that I can't get down the road. That's how it works—your service is thus viewed as a commodity. But hey, if your company is the same as everyone else's, then branded copywriting with your unique brand story isn't necessary. Don't be surprised that you need to keep spending more of those hard-earned dollars on that not-so-round wheel as you try to win over new customers.

Figuring out what makes you unique takes a lot of thought. Be introspective about your true "why," and lay claim to something compelling, outside of the usual notions of being a premier home service provider. Consider your true calling—your mission that your team can get behind. Bottom line: Dig deep. And of course, consider how your visual elements will help personify and be relatable to that story. That's why getting the brand part right is so important.

There are several books to help you find your true calling and vision. One such book is *Traction* by Gino Wickman. What I love about his book is that it helps distill, into its purest form, your company's mission and its "why."

How do you create a brand story that consumers care about? They're interested in much more than how much their plumbing repairs cost or what your guarantee entails. Above all, they want your brand to be authentic. To be real, honest, and also—interesting. They want your messaging to connect with them on a more personal, and even emotional, level. And they want to better understand what makes your brand and, of course, your company unique.

- **Be consistent.** Every time you communicate with a potential customer, your messaging needs to deliver your story in the same consistent fashion. This runs the gamut from how your copywriting is on your collateral and website to how your social media message voice is communicated. It's also how you develop the visuals and imagery used to convey your messages. The more consistent you are, the more your brand wheel will turn and the better your ROI will be on those channels as they work in harmony.

- **Be authentic.** Be true to who you are as a company and keep it real.

- **Be unique.** Identify what makes your company truly unique. That's a hard thing to pinpoint for many companies, but it generally relates back to your "why."

- **Know your audience.** Keep in mind, at all times, who you are talking to. Know what drives and inspires them, and never talk down to them. For home service, nearly 70% of the decision making is done by women.

- **Establish empathy.** Make customers feel something positive about your company, and help them care about you and your team.

- **Voice, tone and content.** It's not just what you say when marketing your company, but how you say it as well. Imagine your brand as a living entity with a specific personality, and then be consistent in the style, mannerisms, and tone of your voice.

Never underestimate the power of a compelling brand story and brand voice. Generally speaking, most of your competitors have none. Which is great news for you.

## Brand voice in branding.

As you consider how to build that perfect brand wheel mentioned earlier, which encompasses all the integration of your brand and its marketing, remember that all those marketing channels that are trying to build your story are also built using a brand voice. The voice is what communicates your story to your audience.

The voice is the personality of your brand. It's how it speaks to the world, and that world includes your external customers and your internal ones: your employees.

# Creating empathy in their community.

After we rebranded **Quality Heating • Cooling • Plumbing** in Tulsa, OK, the owners, Cassie and Oscar Pound, looked for ways to help build on their reputation. At the same time, they wanted to firmly establish themselves as true community partners with a deep appreciation for the homeowners they served. They decided to launch a digital billboard campaign to commemorate special occasions for the people in their communities. Birthdays, anniversaries, and accomplishments were celebrated on their billboards. Of course, their branding was featured, along with the brand colors and assets, but the billboard was primarily about who they served. On social media, the people featured and their families took pictures and shared with everyone they knew, thus continuing to put the brand and the company's purpose in front of many people.

"When we started this billboard campaign, I never imagined it would turn into what it has. I thought people would send us a few birthday shots, etc. We have celebrated weddings, engagements, birthdays, bachelor's degrees, winning sports teams, etc. We even celebrated a day for someone who has passed. The entire campaign has truly helped our company feel proud of the community we serve and it allows us to connect with the amazing people in our community we are blessed to serve." —*Cassie and Oscar Pound*

You might look at it as the theme of your company or its vibe. How does your brand speak and communicate? What are the tone and vibe it gives off? When viewing the channels on that brand wheel, is there a consistent message and theme that it's communicating to the homeowners? And I'm not talking about those lame guarantees and "$59 drain cleaning offers" mentioned earlier. Those aren't brand story elements to use your voice for unless you want to say your brand story revolves around the idea of being a low-cost provider of home service. I doubt most home service companies would consciously want to anchor their story around those types of messages, but many do.

So again, the reality (and opportunity) is that most home service businesses have no unique brand voice that connects at all with either a homeowner or prospective employee. As such, they would have a hard time coming up with a unique characteristic of their voice that defines their brand and integrates into their messaging. Often it's inconsistent, not given much thought, and typically fueled by messages related to pricing, offers, and rebates. None of which truly says much about that company and what makes them unique.

## Branding and ROI.

As mentioned earlier, the idea of your brand wheel spinning efficiently is rooted in the ideas that all your marketing channels are consistently communicating the right messaging and that each touchpoint is on brand. What that means is that no matter where the homeowner interacts with your brand, they understand that the images, styling, and voice are consistent in how they represent your company.

You can think about this in a similar manner to some of the more well-known consumer brands that bombard you with their advertising. Sometimes, it's the first few seconds of a TV ad, and you know exactly what it's an ad for. Sometimes, it's the particular font and how the photos are arranged in a print ad that you immediately can tell which company is being advertised.

The same holds true for home service businesses. And the goal after repetition is to get your brand name top-of-mind for them.

To win their attention, and, more importantly, be remembered when they need your services.

Since home services are not generally considered impulse-type purchases, it's important to think about the long game in your advertising and consistently promote your brand in a way that illustrates the ideals of a positive experience for the homeowner.

This is where home service advertising gets it wrong. Advertising disruption, just for the sake of disruption, does not typically address the idea of becoming "sticky" in a homeowner's mind. That's why pink and purple polka dots for your truck wrap are not a good idea. Yes, your brand is noticed, but no—it doesn't help consumers believe you will give them a favorable experience. (We'll expand upon advertising disruption in chapter 3.)

Every instance and medium that you deploy your brand in must be consistent to maximize the ROI on your overall spend. If we don't get that foundation right (the hub of that wheel), then none of those opportunities can be maximized for the best ROI.

Consider your truck wraps, for example. Without that solid logo, you can't build an effective truck wrap design, and thus, your ROI is compromised. We have data to support the effectiveness of the companies whose fleets we've rebranded, compared to the old one. Some of the stats are staggering in terms of effectiveness— sometimes as high as 16x revenue compared to prior branding. Some generated huge increases in calls tied directly to the vehicles.

But it's not just how the branding on vehicles can generate more specific calls. It's about how each of the impressions those vehicles make contribute to the overall marketing on other channels, like your digital marketing.

## Buehler? Buehler? Buehler?

The rebranding of Jacksonville, FL-based Buehler Air perfectly illustrates how being remarkable in one's market helps those businesses make the most of their advertising budget. In 2019, we spoke to Jason Buehler about rebranding and renaming his business.

At the time, it was called Air Source America, which is a great name if you supply oxygen to people, but maybe not so great a name for a heating and air conditioning company. After almost a decade of very slow growth (5%-10% per year), Jason knew something wasn't working. From an operational standpoint, he was doing a lot of great things. He had amazing reviews, great processes and procedures, and good employees.

But the core problem was no one could remember the name of his company, but they all remembered his last name, due to the notoriety of the movie *Ferris Bueller's Day Off*. Normally, renaming your business after your last name is a really bad idea (see chapter 4), but in this case, we thought it would make sense to create a fun brand to go along with his memorable last name.

What were the results? In one year, they went from $2.5 million to $5 million. After two years, they were already at $7 million plus. And in year three, they exceeded $10 million.

What changed here? In a nutshell, he went from *blanding* his business to *branding* it. He became remarkable in his community by building a remarkable brand. A brand that people remembered, that connected to the homeowners. And the tagline "Stay Cooler with Buehler" worked perfectly with the imagery of the big, giant "cool" head we designed for the logo and truck wrap.

Many will insist that to grow fast, you need to spend a large percentage of revenue on advertising. Many suggest numbers of 10% or more to grow. Of course, the weaker the branding is, the more those companies will spend to see results. But the beauty of great branding is that you don't need nearly as much money for marketing to grow because the branding does so much work on its own.

## The fact remains that weak brands will always need more money to gain traction.

**In the case of Buehler, all his growth was achieved by spending less than 4% of revenue on marketing.** How is that possible? How many coaches would insist that number should be at least doubled for growth? It's always surprising to me that no one looks first at the brand before deciding the number you need to spend. And while I understand that different markets may be more expensive to market a service business, the fact remains that weak brands will always need more money to gain traction.

Later we'll talk more in detail about how brands and truck wraps are a critical part of brand building. But in the case of Buehler Air, the results are quite remarkable and illustrate how critical it is to get the branding and wrap design right. In 2021, $1 million in revenue was attributed to their 18 wrapped trucks. If you figure that 18 wrapped trucks cost about $72,000 and last about five years, then we can figure the amortized cost to be $14,400 per year. I'm pretty sure there is no other advertising medium generating a 70x return on that investment.

This is part of what we call "winning on the streets" because the name itself has become top-of-mind to the homeowners who need Buehler's service, due to the visibility of the trucks in the community. By having his trucks more *disruptive* (see chapter 3), he has garnered

attention and made his brand stickier in the minds of the people he is targeting. That means his digital marketing is working better, because he's getting so many branded searches instead of hoping he's number one for "Jacksonville air conditioning repair."

## Every impression matters.

That wheel we spoke about early in the chapter has many spokes that comprise it. Each spoke is important to make that wheel turn efficiently and deliver a maximum ROI on your marketing spend. That means that controlling how your brand communicates to the homeowners at every single touchpoint is crucial. Every message needs to be on-brand, every time.

# CHAPTER 2

# WHEN IS IT TIME TO REBRAND?

# Knowing the time to change course.

For existing businesses, there is a good chance that a rebrand for your home service business is in your best interests and a wise investment to make. But knowing when to abandon your current brand and build a better brand is a huge decision. There are so many variables to weigh out.

If you are a new business hiring professionals to brand your company and start you out on the right foot, congratulations. You made a very good decision. But for the majority of growing businesses, a brand is typically something that wasn't given a lot of thought from the start. Perhaps it was something that was rushed through because you needed to get out there as soon as possible and start trying to make some money. Maybe today, it no longer reflects who the company is or what it represents.

## Brand inconsistencies and brand dilution.

Many growing home service businesses have never been given any type of brand identity guidebook or standard to illustrate how their brand should be integrated across various media. Most large ad agencies provide a lengthy brand style guide that illustrates how your brand should be used and, more importantly, how it should not be used. But the reality is that most small businesses do not have such a document. Generally, they have a few file formats of their logo, which they share with various people working on their marketing materials. Maybe they know their brand colors and, if they're lucky, which fonts should be used with their marketing materials.

Maybe the owner of the wrap company gets a copy of the logo file and does his thing and adds his spin to the design. Then the magazine and web designers get their copies, and they decide to be "creative." What ultimately happens is that each of them has a different interpretation of your brand implementation. Perhaps the magazine creates an ad and the headline is one font. The web designer creates your homepage animation using a different font and decides to change the font for your tagline. One of your employees decides that the font for your company would look better yet another way. You get the picture.

## Sometimes a brand doesn't represent what a company has become—or where it hopes to go.

Over some time, your brand is diluted due to these inconsistencies. There is no consistent brand identity since nothing has been established as a guideline. If you have a single-source agency coordinating your marketing, this should never happen. Essentially they become the gatekeeper of your brand. But for those who rely on many different vendors, it is almost impossible to achieve consistent brand application, especially in the absence of a brand style guide.

But if you remember the wheel we spoke about in chapter 1, we're suddenly building a marketing plan that is already not going to spin right because now your touchpoints to the homeowner are inconsistent and confusing.

When you look across your marketing efforts, is it clear that they present a consistent picture of your brand? At a glance, do all materials have a branded look that allows people to "see" the connection between applications? If the materials do not share that common denominator, it's a good time to re-examine your brand architecture and consider a brand update or refresh.

# Rebranding is the catalyst for positive change.

All these companies at one point thought they had a great brand. Then they realized their brand no longer represented who they were and where they wanted to go.

**108%** INCREASE IN REVENUE

GEE! HEATING & AIR
770-282-4930
GeeHVAC.com

**6 MONTHS** AFTER REBRANDING

**112%** INCREASE IN REVENUE

ideal temp HEATING & COOLING
IdealTempKC.com

**1 YEAR** AFTER REBRANDING

**1133%** INCREASE IN REVENUE

Hansen HEATING & AIR

**6 YEARS** AFTER REBRANDING

**137%** INCREASE IN REVENUE

Seatown
seatownservices.com

**2 YEARS** AFTER REBRANDING

**53%** INCREASE IN REVENUE

QUALITY HEATING. COOLING. PLUMBING
Quality-HC.com
918-518-5900

**6 MONTHS** AFTER REBRANDING

**619%** INCREASE IN REVENUE

G.I.PLUMBING
GIPlumbing.com
412-977-8691

**1 YEAR** AFTER REBRANDING

## Branding that doesn't represent you.

If your business is like most businesses, it has probably grown over the years. Perhaps the services or products have evolved or changed. Maybe you've added plumbing and electrical to your HVAC company or decided to focus on solar after starting primarily in electric.

As a result of your evolution, your core target audience may have changed over the years, and your primary sales focus may have also changed. So the question to ask yourself is: Has your brand kept up with these changes?

Sometimes a brand doesn't represent what a company has become— or where it hopes to go. Maybe the brand was never good to begin with and now that the business is growing and trying to attract higher-paying customers, it doesn't quite look the part. The brand identity is holding them back from achieving their full potential. When a company seeks to compete with the big boys as a market player, an amateur brand is like an anchor around its neck. Yet many home service businesses allow a small measure of success to keep that anchor in place. (Chapter 3 details some of those fears that hold owners back from moving forward.)

## The question to ask yourself is: Has your brand kept up with these changes?

When a brand ceases to represent you or speak to your target audience in a meaningful way, it's time to give serious consideration to a fresh start. It's only going to get more expensive the longer you wait.

## Is your branding attracting the right employees?

Does the brand speak to the high-caliber employee you want to attract to your open positions? Or does the company look dated and uninspiring from visual and cultural perspectives? Without employees, you can't sell to homeowners. Be introspective and take a hard look at what signals your branding is sending to candidates.

## Brand-name confusion in the market.

We've seen many examples of similarly named companies operating within the same market, and each company cannibalizes the others' marketing efforts. Being able to own your brand name in your market is huge. Think about all the branded searches you want homeowners to do after seeing your trucks in their community. If there is a similarly named competitor also benefiting from those efforts, obviously you're wasting your advertising dollars.

## Revenue and rebranding.

I'm often asked about revenue as it relates to rebranding. The most common school of thought from home service owners as they get larger is that they are too large to rebrand or that it will be too costly to rebrand. Chapter 3 will debunk this in greater detail, but we've spanned the revenue gamut of rebranding—with companies as little as a few hundred thousand dollars all the way up to $100 million in revenue. The smaller your company, the more nimble you are to pivot for a rebrand. It's cheaper to redo all your "stuff" simply because you own less of it. It's less traumatic, to a certain extent, and it's probably easier from a logistical perspective. But make no mistake—the longer you live with a poor brand, the more expensive it is. So if you think it's expensive to rebrand a $10 million company, wait until you're a $20 million company. But the real cost isn't just in the number of things that need to be changed—it's in the cost of missed opportunities and spending more on your marketing.

It's not uncommon for larger companies to get scared of rebranding. We've had a few examples of building amazing rebrands for bigger companies, only for them to get cold feet when they realized that it was going to be actual work to implement and some hard costs to integrate. Often, it's the fleet rebranding that scares them. So they continue with their awful brands, all because they're afraid to make the investment now and do the work it takes to roll it out. And they kick the can down the street. They don't care; they're still making money. But it remains a missed opportunity they don't grasp.

If I look at the last several hundred rebrands we've been a part of, I can't think of a single instance of a rebrand that didn't yield an amazing ROI. Either move forward or get out of the way. If you do plan to stay complacent with a poor brand, just know there are other companies in your space hiring companies like us who do understand the value of a great home service brand and who will start taking some of your market shares. Oh, and I hope you don't mind overspending on your marketing, either. If you think rebranding is expensive, not rebranding is usually even more expensive. You just don't realize it. More on that later.

## Hallmarks of a poor brand.

For most home service businesses, their brand was never professionally designed in the first place. As such, it may exhibit some common amateurish elements generally used by people with little brand experience.

- **Your logo has a swoosh, beveled Photoshop effect, etc.** If your logo has a swoosh or any type of Photoshop effect added to the type, you definitely have a poor logo. There is a mathematical certainty to this rule, and there are absolutely no exceptions. It would take a second book to explain why, so just trust me. Yes, I know that Nike has a swoosh. That doesn't count. Photoshop effects are a clear sign of an amateur brand created by an amateur designer. Swooshes went out in the late '90s when every new brand had one. Your designer forgot to check their inbox for the memo.

- **Your logo contains red and blue arrows or a flame and snowflake combo.** This is yet another mathematical certainty. There is no chance your red and blue arrows will ever be unique enough to own and represent your company, nor will the lame

# A1 from day 1, but never complacent.

"I realized that my old logo and wrap didn't pop. There was no color scheme, no story, and it wasn't a clear message. Then I realized my website, my site signs, sticker, mailer—nothing stood out. The new brand is just so good, and it makes people feel good about us. After rebranding, sales went up dramatically. People recognized the trucks and branding became solidified. From a consistency standpoint, now everything matches and delivers brand promise.

"When your brand is disjointed and you don't have a clean look, it hurts sales; it hurts culture and recruitment. Customers don't respect the company nearly as much. When we pull up to a customer's house, it's a targeted message. We demand a higher price. If you want a pristine service, done the right way, with a company that is going to honor your warranty, you call A1. And when you walk in here, it's a place where people enjoy working and the brand has a lot to do with that.

"We've grown a lot organically and through acquisitions, and revenue is up over $110 million since rebranding." **—Tommy Mello, A1 Garage, Phoenix, AZ**

*Tommy and me at his Phoenix shop.*

flame and snowflake graphic. If you have them in your logo, yeah, it's probably time. Cut it loose. You can thank me later.

- **Your logo contains a photo.** If your logo contains an image that is photographed rather than illustrated, you have a brand that won't work for many applications. It means that the logo is bitmap-based rather than vector-based. The difference between the two is that vector-based logos are infinitely scalable, regardless of whether they are used on a billboard or T-shirt. Bitmap-based logos lose quality as they are made larger.

- **Your logo is illegible from a distance.** Many graphic designers do not design well for outdoor use or fully appreciate the importance for small businesses that rely upon signage or vehicle advertising. Often, you see a logo that works fine in print or online but fails in an outdoor realm. Ironically, if a logo works well from a distance-legibility standpoint, it must work well for print and online applications.

- **Your logo uses generic clip art.** While it's certainly possible to have a decent logo that uses clip art, there is nothing that prevents a competitor from using the same clip art in their logo. It also means your logo can never be trademarked. If the logo includes tired clip art that's been used a hundred times for similar business types, its value is severely diluted. This is especially true of the popular clip art mascots that you see over and over again. There is nothing stopping anyone in your market from using the same mascot. I find it almost hilarious that one of the larger HVAC companies in the country uses generic clip art for their logo. Anyone in their market could use the same logo and they'd be untouchable from a legal standpoint.

- **Your logo was created using a template.** If your logo was created online using a logo template site or with logo template software, there is a high likelihood that it has little value for your business. It will employ generic clip art that probably won't represent your business in a unique and meaningful way. There also may not be any logic about how to carry that particular logo into all required media, which is a critical deficiency.

- **Your logo has a meaningless icon.** In general, meaningless icons don't work for home service businesses. These businesses usually rely on media formats that do not allow viewers time to study the icon and discern the nature of the business. Small businesses also don't have the luxury of spending millions of dollars on advertising to get people to understand the meaning of their icon or connect it with their business type. They're almost impossible to build a meaningful brand story around.

- **Your logo looks dated.** Sometimes a brand just looks old. Not retro old (in a good way), but late '80s or '90s dated-old. The typography seems dated, or the illustrative style and graphics seem dated. This presents a challenge when developing new marketing materials that are supposed to look modern or cutting-edge. A dated brand may hamstring your efforts to produce a fresh, up-to-date look for your marketing materials. If your brand looks like it's stuck in the '80s, it is difficult to make it look relevant.

- **Your logo contains a mascot that looks like it could beat the crap out of you.** Do I really need to state why this is a bad idea? If your mascot looks like he's all muscled and aggressively running toward you while carrying an oversize wrench that could be used as a weapon, you might want to think about the signal that sends to Mrs. Jones, who is already scared shitless about who she lets in her house.

You may be thinking, "Well, thanks for trashing my current brand. After my therapy sessions are over, then what?"

Now that we've maybe crushed your dreams about the validity of your existing brand, let's go deeper into the logistics of what your brand should be doing, outside of the potential issues we've noted. Because there's more to it than just needing a pretty logo, not using lame clip art, and having legible lettering. Oh, and those pesky psychotic-looking mascots. Let's talk more about the psychology behind building a brand that works.

CHAPTER 3

# WHAT IS BRAND DISRUPTION?

# Pardon the interruption.

Disruption became a more common term in the last decade. Often it was used to describe businesses that disrupted a particular industry by doing something different than what everyone else was doing. Uber and Lyft are good examples of industry disruptors. When it comes to branding, disruption has a dual goal: to look at what everyone else is doing as far as branding is concerned and to find a way to be unique while still communicating a positive brand promise.

In his book *Purple Cow,* Seth Godin talks about driving through the countryside and seeing the same cows over and over, and how the sheer abundance of commonality among them makes them unremarkable. But what happens if during that drive, after seeing hundreds of identical black and white cows, you suddenly saw a purple cow? That purple cow would capture your attention; you would certainly notice it.

The same is true with branding, especially for home service businesses. The consumer you are trying to attract is being bombarded with literally hundreds, if not thousands, of ads and images that are vying for their attention: from signage and billboards to vehicles. And of course, it's not just when they leave the house; it's on their computers, TVs, and phones. All advertising is designed to penetrate the psyche and become sticky.

This is the primary reason why your fleet branding is critical. Think of your vans as the cows dotting the countryside. Most of them, sadly, look the same.

All those black and white cows are similar to the branding strategies of the vast majority of home service businesses. They all tend to blend in or ... bland. Many suffer from the horrible calamity known as WVS or White Van Syndrome. The idea of disruption is the cure for that affliction. Think about how many commercial vehicles you see every day in your community. How many blend, and how many cause you to take a second look? Does your truck blend in with the rest of them?

Sometimes, because you are so close to your own brand, you don't even realize that it blends in. Several years ago, we had the opportunity to rebrand Blanton's Heating and Air in Fayetteville, NC. The owner, Will Blanton, had been sitting at a traffic light when one of his existing vans drove by, as did several competitors' vans. And he realized that none of them stood out. It was one of those epiphanies when he understood he was suffering from WVS. We rebranded his company with a fun mascot and a purple and grey color scheme, making him unique in the market and helping him to grow from $3.5 million to $28 million in the nine years since rebranding.

## Are you truly ready to be different?

Will Blanton wasn't of the mindset to embrace the status quo or think his current success was a sound strategy to help him move the needle faster to where he wanted to go. Neither was Ken Goodrich when he came to us to help rebrand Goettl in 2013. He knew the existing Goettl brand wasn't going to get him to where he needed to go. He leveraged the opportunity he saw to build a great brand story and gain an advantage over his competitors, who were quite comfortable with the status quo. In 2021, Goettl earned over $250 million in revenue. That market share came at the expense of his competitors' complacency.

We tend to look at the complacency so prevalent in home service branding as the best opportunity most businesses have to gain market share and be disruptive. In fact, there is nothing I love seeing more than weak brands in our clients' markets. It's awesome because it's much easier to make a disruptive brand in those markets.

Why is the idea of investing in branding foreign to so many "successful" companies? There are plenty of reasons, but we have to put a disclaimer on how we describe "successful." One can argue that their "success" nullifies the theory that branding is important. Look at how "successful" they were with their awful brands. Doesn't that prove that branding isn't all that important? Well, let's look at it another way. Can you imagine how much more successful they might have been if they had a better branding strategy? Imagine how much money they might have saved on advertising if they had a better brand. Or how much higher their average tickets might have been if people felt they were buying from a premium brand.

**Anyone can spend their way out of a poor brand. Let's leave that to your competitors.**

One needs to realize that you can always try to spend your way out of bad branding, but there remains one simple, undeniable truth: The poorer the brand, the more money you will spend on advertising. In the words of Roy H. Williams, "Overspending on marketing is the tax that businesses spend for being unremarkable."

The fact is that's how so many home service businesses get by and are even "successful" with poor brands. They need to overspend on their marketing because their brands are quite unremarkable. They're forgettable, and because they don't break through the clutter and aren't disruptive, the people they are trying to reach ultimately don't care about what they have to sell.

# "Overspending on marketing is the tax that businesses spend for being unremarkable."

Must companies increase their marketing spend to get the phone ringing more? There is a lot of chatter about how much advertising a home service business should spend as a percentage of revenue. The typical range is 0%-15%. For the folks who spend nothing, they typically explain that word of mouth is enough for them. Generally speaking, those aren't businesses in growth mode; they're more likely in status-quo mode. And for those who spend more than 12%, they usually say that figure is required in their particular market to grow.

Often when I hear someone quote those high percentages on a Facebook page for home service company owners, I stalk their profiles to see what company they work for. Inevitably, it becomes as clear as day why they need to spend so much of their revenue on advertising: Their brand is unremarkable.

So what do most businesses usually do? They spend more than they would if they had a better brand. Different markets may necessitate different spends, but isn't the goal to spend the least amount of money while still achieving high growth? A brand is foundational to the success of any marketing campaign. If Kmart had decided one day to sell high-end computers to go head to head with Apple, do you think they would have stood a chance with their existing brand? It's really not much different in home service. The better the brand, the easier it is to sell a premium product. There is nothing revolutionary about this concept; it's common sense.

Of course, you also have some businesses with poor brands that manage to experience great growth numbers while spending very little. Those are the ones I love to rebrand because you know they are killing it operationally to achieve that growth. Now we just need to add some gasoline to the fire and blow it up with the right marketing. Tom Howard from Lee's Air is a good example of someone who saw

the benefits of elevating his "crap" brand (his words, not mine). "We had a growth rate just under 40% last year: $17.3 million to $24 million. I can't say it was all from branding but what I can say is that we pretty accurately forecast our call volume each year. **Based on our marketing spend, though, we generated 50% more calls than we would have expected with the same marketing spend.** In the busy season, we were shocked and we got seriously short-handed in our customer service department and have never been that far off on our forecast. The only thing I can attribute it to is our branding. It helps lift all of your campaigns."

## If it ain't broke, don't fix it—except when it is broke and you just don't know it.

Change requires courage. Every business is a work in progress, and no one should ever believe that anything they are doing today is good enough for tomorrow. That is what separates good companies from great companies. But many simply don't know what they don't know.

I tend to look at business owners' sometimes irrational affinity for their existing brand as Warm Blanket Syndrome. It's all soft and comforting. It's reassuring. It's what got them this far. But is it working? Most think it's working fine because they don't know the difference between branding and blanding.

I can add myself to this list as well. I had a brand and a name that I used for 22 years. It seemed like it was working—sort of. The name I started with was Graphic D-Signs, because way back then I did some signs and lettering as well as traditional graphic design. But that was not what we became 22 years later. We no longer did anything with signs, and we were so much more than a graphic design company.

I knew many years before we renamed and rebranded that it was time. But I was resistant to the idea of change. For a branding guy, that might seem strange. Rebranding is hard work. It means doing a lot of stuff over. It costs money. You need new brochures, signage, website, trademark filings, banking, and remarketing to

# The biggest surprise?
# Rebranding is hard work.

"Rebranding has been the single best business decision I've made in the last 10 years. While that is a bold statement, I firmly believe that rebranding allowed us to make the impact we've had in our market and gain recognition along with the other well-established companies in town.

"The main reason was that we wanted to refresh our image and disrupt our market with a new look. Our old logo was bland and didn't capture the essence of our company. We needed something that would help us look like a much larger company. Something that showed customers when we arrived at their home or when driving around town that we were a professional company. I hear from co-workers and customers that we have the best branding in town and people now recognize and love our house logo.

"The biggest surprise we discovered after rebranding was just how much work it is! There's a lot that goes into changing your identity and disrupting a market with a significant amount of competitors.

"In 2019 we ended the year at $1.3 million in revenue. We rebranded in April 2020 and ended 2020 at $5.5 million. In 2021 we ended the year at $12.3 million. This phenomenal growth could not have happened without a strong brand to carry our message and disrupt our market. It has benefited us in several other areas, as we've had employees who said they wanted to work for Balanced Comfort because they were interested in driving the best-looking vans in town." **—Aaron Husak, CEO, Balanced Comfort, Fresno, CA**

customers. But deep down I knew we needed to change. I used the building of our new office as the catalyst for that decision. Thus, KickCharge™ Creative was born.

Now I am glad we went through with it. Otherwise, I doubt we'd have had the growth we experienced or that we would have attracted the right talent to continue to grow. More importantly, the rebrand helped us attract the right kind of client. It also gave me a deeper understanding of why so many home service business owners are reluctant to change.

**Here are some of those reasons that I've seen:**

- **Warm blankets.** As discussed earlier, old brands can be very comforting, and they seem to be working, so why change? Which leads me to…

- **Afraid of change.** Change is hard. It means accepting the notion that you might not be doing something the right way. It means knowing that what got you here today may not be good enough to get you where you want to go in the future. We love working with clients whose biggest competitors are complacent and essentially standing still because they lack the courage to implement change. That screams opportunity to me! Let's pounce while they marvel at their own "greatness."

- **It's hard work to execute.** Yes, it certainly is. You know what's easy? Not changing. Complacency is easy. It doesn't require any work. But is standing still a sound business strategy for the future? If you're not moving forward, you're going backward. And as you continue to grow, it gets harder and harder, and you become deeper ensconced in the old brand. Many larger companies suffer from this, not understanding that the hard work today pays dividends later.

- **Branding is so expensive!** The irony of waiting to change your brand is how much money is wasted while you wait. The longer you wait to do things the right way, the more expensive the endeavor becomes. The bigger you grow and the more things you have branded, the more expensive it becomes to change. The most common refrain we hear is "Man, I wish I had done this sooner." I recently spoke at a trade show where I talked with the owner of a plumbing company that was earning $15 million in revenue. The brand was awful, with a super aggressive mascot who looked like he might beat the shit out of someone. I talked about rebranding, and he said, "It's too expensive to rebrand now." To which I replied, "Well, dude, it sure as hell isn't going to be cheaper at $20 million."

Remember, it's not just the actual cost of rebranding you have to factor in. It's the cost of *not* rebranding. How many opportunities were missed? How many sales didn't close? The least expensive time to rebrand is yesterday, not tomorrow.

- **Success in spite of a poor brand is not a valid reason to perpetuate it.** I wrote this quote many years ago, and I loved it so much that we had a big sign made for the office.

The success one achieves becomes a good rationale for not examining what might have been possible with a better brand. So, owners become blinded by the existing success, instead of truly thinking deeply about how a better image would help them achieve even greater success.

- **Don't know their brand is poor.** Let's face it: Who is going to be the one to tell you that your brand is poor? Do you think your employees will? Your spouse? Those are the very people who are most afraid of change. Will the sign company tell you when they wrap your truck? Or the screen printer? Or the web company? Or the media buyer? Those are the very people who should tell you, but often, little thought is given to the foundation, and they're told, "Here's our logo—please create some advertising." Telling a potential client that their logo sucks won't endear the owners to them. I'm blessed to not suffer from this lack of tact. If your logo sucks, I'm going to tell you. If you're unsure if your branding is poor or deficient in any way graphically, shoot me an email, and I'll be happy to tell you the truth. I'm not interested in you continuing to waste money on campaigns that are destined to be marginalized by poor branding. I truly believe that no marketing company should

# Plomero creates its own purple cow.

"After being in a one-man crew, owning my business for 10 years, and overspending in marketing year after year trying to compete with all the big players in my already competitive market, I realized I had to make a change and a big one! My branding was so bad that my family didn't know the name of my company. It took me two years to finally pull the trigger to fully rebrand, and my only regret now is not doing it sooner. I went from spending 20% of my advertising budget to 5%, as most of my leads come organically now. From a one-man crew to a team of five now, having a great brand gives our company a great advantage.

"Immediately after the rebrand, my company took a 180-degree turn. The impact on my community after my two trucks hit the road was incredible. The amount of calls we get from only having two trucks on the road is incredible; our customers say they see our trucks all the time and think we are a huge company. Culture and recruitment took a big spin as well. We had never received a phone call from someone looking for employment before. Now we get two or three employment inquiries a month. My only piece of advice is to be ready for the aftermath, as growth and demand come to you very quickly after you rebrand.

"Before rebranding: one-man crew, $300,000 in revenue. After rebranding: one technician, one apprentice, $648,000 in revenue. Our goal for next year is to hit $1 million." **—Armando Ramos, Plomero en Phoenix, Phoenix, AZ**

take money from clients and deliver creative services they know won't work. But hey, that's just me.

- **Don't understand the effect of ROI.** We'll talk more about ROI and branding later, but the bottom line is that most owners don't understand the relationship between branding and their marketing ROI. As such, most are content to continue spending more and more as their ROI keeps shrinking while failing to see the root cause of that lack of ROI. The weak brand is an anchor they're dragging around.

- **Their ego.** So much ego is wrapped up in the existing branding that, many owners can't fathom the idea that it's hurting their business. I get why you love your logo. I truly do. Maybe your wife did it, or your nephew, or your buddy "who is really good at Photoshop." Just consider the possibility that it does suck. Without fail, the most successful brands we've created were for owners with no egos. Trust the experts, and let them get on with what they do. In the words of Joe Crisara, the legendary HVAC sales coach, "Your ego is not your amigo."

## Purple cows are unique, but that's only half the battle.

Godin was on to something for sure when he talked about how purple cows stood out in the countryside. The cows are like your trucks, and we want them to stand out. But disruption is not enough. When building a brand, there needs to be more to it than just standing out. Go wrap your trucks with pink and purple polka dots, and I guarantee you—they will stand out. But the big question is: What does your pink-and-purple-polka-dot-branded vehicle say about your company?

Many companies forget that you need to disrupt while simultaneously delivering the brand promise to the viewer. First, we capture their attention; then we help deliver an idea of who you are and what they can expect to get if they hire you. That's the knockout punch. They see and remember you, and they have an idea of what kind of company you are.

Far too often I hear owners talk about their current trucks. "People say they see our trucks all the time!" Cool story. What they generally don't talk about is what those impressions fail to deliver. You could put 100 vans in any given community and people would say they see those vans all the time. But do they deliver a message beyond that impression? Most don't deliver a positive brand promise and message. At best, most are completely neutral, and the rest leave a negative impression.

## The real beauty of disruptive branding.

What's awesome about disruptive brand strategies is that they are still not widely embraced. Generally speaking, in most markets where we are asked to rebrand a company, there rarely is another well-branded company in their space. There may be more well-known companies, but don't confuse notoriety with good branding. As I mentioned earlier, some of the largest companies in the home service space have some of the worst brands.

Additionally, you often see home service companies offer no authentic brand story to complement their marketing messaging. Or you see vague unique selling propositions (USPs) that have become so common that they're no longer unique. You see them used in weak taglines that almost any other competitor could use. They feature trite and vague promises associated with "guarantees" or common phrases like "honesty and integrity." None of those things speak to consumers because they are brand story ideas and concepts that can't be uniquely owned. And since so many other companies make similar claims, consumers believe none of them. As such, they're not disruptive. If you've seen the movie *Tommy Boy*, you know that the guarantee is worth about as much as the box it's printed on—or, in this case, the truck wrap.

On some level, I can't fault some of these companies who never graduate beyond their weak and unremarkable brands. As I said earlier, you don't know what you don't know. But it is odd in some respects. There has probably never been more publicity about branding than there is today. They really should know better, especially if they're astute about how consumer behavior is related to purchasing decisions.

When you consider how much big consumer-product companies spend on branding and advertising their products, it's ironic that the majority of the home service industry has not caught on to the importance of branding and brand presentation. Branding is about a company getting people to believe something about the potential buying experience and encouraging them to choose a certain brand by attracting their attention.

Selling home service is not radically different from selling consumer products. Consider this analogy: If your home service were a package on a shelf in a supermarket, what would you do to attract the attention of the shopper? Maybe you'd deploy colorful graphics and an attractive package design that looked premium. You'd invest heavily in something to hopefully connect with the consumer and make them believe that your product is better than the 10 similar products sitting on the shelves. But most home service companies don't think this way as it relates to their brand, and the consumer ultimately has no chance to distinguish the buying experience. It's like walking down an aisle where every package is almost the same color, with the same fonts and the same size. Like a sea of red and blue arrows or an orange sun and snowflakes. A more appropriate comparison might be a sea of white vans. They all look the same. And once consumers have seen 100 vans that look almost the same to them, they ignore them all.

What that means for us can be summed up in one word: opportunity. There are so many ways in which the playing field has been leveled for running a successful home service. There are similar software programs, similar pricing strategies, and similar digital marketing tactics. But in a lot of markets, branding remains an untapped opportunity to capitalize on your competitors' weaknesses. As I mentioned earlier, often the bigger they are, the more complacent they are as it relates to their branding, and therefore the bigger the opportunity for you to leverage their weakness.

Let's crush them while they're basking in their mediocrity and leave them wondering how you just managed to take a bunch of their market share. Let's exploit their complacency and leverage it to our advantage. *Now that is fun!*

## Win on the streets so you can win online.

Chapter 7 goes into more detail about the role effective wrap design has on your overall strategy, but it's important to talk about the idea of disruption on the streets to better understand the opportunity it presents to home service companies.

Take a look at the chart below, from Invoca.com in 2021, which identifies how many consumers did not have one company in mind when searching online. If you look at the numbers, they scream **opportunity**.

The funny thing is that most people misinterpret this data to prove how important it is to invest in SEO for unbranded keywords. But what are they missing in the numbers? This isn't the data to prove how important it is to invest in SEO. It's quite the opposite. This data proves how important it is to invest in branding and to be top-of-mind. You don't want people searching for "heating repair Staten Island"; rather, you'd like them to search for your brand name instead.

That is how disruption should work. You work toward making your brand name sticky by being memorable, not fitting in. Do you still need SEO? Of course you do. But I can tell you if you win on the streets first, you'll need to invest less in SEO. Don't forget this fundamental truth: **The more your brand becomes a household name, the less money you need to spend to market it.** And of course, **the weaker the brand, the more money it costs to market it**.

## Percent of Consumers that did <u>not</u> have one company in mind when searching

| | | | |
|---|---|---|---|
| **80%** Appliance Repair | **74%** Carpet Cleaning | **83%** Decks & Patios | **90%** Electrical |
| **68%** Home Remodeling | **90%** House Cleaning | **84%** HVAC Repair | **80%** Lawn Care |
| **86%** Painting | **83%** Pest Control | **76%** Plumbing | **80%** Roofing |

(LSA)

# CHAPTER 4

# NAMING

*Before renaming.*

# The foundation for building your brand.

A business name should make people feel something positive about your business if they don't know anything about it. And it should be easy to remember. Great names do both. However, most home service company names will do neither. Get your naming wrong, and once again, you'll have to spend more money to overcome the deficiency.

I'm addressing two types of readers: startup owners who are looking to launch a brand and existing business owners who already have a brand and are trying to build a better one. Each one has different needs, but of course, much of the foundational advice is the same as it relates to branding.

If you're venturing off to launch a new home service business, you have a clean slate as it relates to branding. From creative and brand story perspectives, that means we're unlimited in how we build a disruptive brand. We can build everything from the ground up with a solid foundation, and your business will hit the market with all the right tools and a consistent look and feel. Doing branding correctly at the beginning is the most cost-effective way to launch your business, even if funds are limited. It's probably the smartest investment you can make because it means you won't have to address brand deficiencies later on, which is so much more costly. Redoing your signage, your truck wraps, your uniforms, and your website: All have to be considered later on if not done correctly initially.

## Should you rename your home service brand?

For those with an existing business, you'll bring with you some baggage. You already have a business name, a logo, and perhaps a host of things integrating everything. Perhaps there is even some recognition of your brand in your community, although most contractors grossly overestimate how much brand recognition they have. But assessing whether or not a makeover makes sense is dependent on several factors. Here are a few to consider:

- **How long have you been in business?** Longevity plays a role in assessing brand equity, and potential recognition within the community. Generally speaking the longer you've been in business, the more equity you may have. However, just being an older company doesn't necessarily mean that you can't make a change.

- **How well known are your brand and brand name in your market?** This is sometimes hard to judge. Sometimes you see last-name-based brands that have a fair amount of equity in their brand name, assuming the owner and company are active within the community. But most have less brand equity than they think, especially if the branding is weak on their trucks.

- **Revenue.** The smaller the company, the more nimble they are. It's much easier to rename and rebrand a company with revenue under a few million than it is if they are over $20 million. That said, we've still done many rebranding and renaming efforts for contractors in that range, and all have grown dramatically afterward. Again, we shed the weight of a poor name and built a better, stickier brand to grow with. However, keep in mind that the revenue size will correlate with the expenses needed to rebrand and with all the marketing that uses the old brand. There are more trucks to rewrap, more uniforms to buy and so on compared to a smaller company.

Those are some of the logistics when considering renaming and rebranding. The other considerations are more about the name itself and what the name speaks to or, rather, doesn't speak to. Here are some additional considerations as you weigh the pros and cons of renaming your company:

- **Is the name hard to spell or pronounce?** I'm always surprised to see names for home service businesses that are hard to pronounce or even harder to spell. This negatively affects so many things in your marketing channel. Recently we had a client with a difficult name who shared some of his radio spots with me. Upon hearing the spot, I realized there was no way I would know how to spell the name. This is especially troublesome when you consider the importance of organic branded searches. How would you expect someone to find you online with a branded search when they can't even spell your name? Often you see this issue with last-name-based brands.

- **Is the name based on a last name?** Last-name brands are generally not a good idea. If you are starting out, then we would say to never name your business after yourself. If you've been using it a long time and are well known in your community, then you have to decide if keeping a last-name brand is worth it for the long-term growth and the ability to be sticky in a consumer's mind. The big challenge with last-name brands is their lack of brand promise, which we'll discuss in greater detail.

- **Does the name use initials?** By far, one of the worst names you could have for a home service brand is one that uses random initials like CBK Heating and Air or P&C Mechanical. You will spend thousands upon thousands of dollars trying to get people to remember your name. What's worse, for those who do remember it, none of them will have any idea of your brand promise from just hearing your name. Certain initial-based names work, like Tommy Mello's A1 Garage, because there is an associated value placed on being "A1." But most initial-based brands mean nothing to the average consumer. There's no expectation of service, no natural visual elements to connect the name to the brand, and little chance of ever building an effective brand story.

The company that has been cutting my grass for the last 15 years has a name with initials. They park a 16-foot enclosed trailer in front of my house every week. There is a huge logo with their initials on it. It's legible, has a few leaves, and says "Landscaping" under those initials. What's the name?

I can't tell you. I think there is an A in the name, like AGK Landscaping, but that's not their name. And I'm a guy who studies logos for a living. Do you think most homeowners are paying any attention to a meaningless brand name that uses initials? What reason would they ever have for remembering such an unremarkable name?

- **Is the name based on a location?** The theory of naming your business based on a location is rooted in the idea that being local is an advantage that homeowners will care about. Sometimes they do care about you being local. The problem comes when you try to sell home service outside the area you're named after. It essentially handcuffs you to a service area. We renamed and rebranded Antioch Heating and Air a few years back due to this very challenge. No one outside Antioch thought they serviced their area. Their new name, Comfort Cavalry, has had remarkable success since rebranding, and they were able to penetrate new markets outside Antioch. Be cautious when choosing names based on locations, especially if you hope to expand one day.

- **Are there companies in your market with names that sound similar?** We've repeatedly seen this issue arise. And one would think the states would do a better job of monitoring this or helping to avoid similar names in the state. But as long as there are slight variances in spelling or an additional word or two added to a name, that company is typically not going to be flagged when it files its LLC or S-Corp. Thus, the potential for very similar-sounding names exists in markets. If that is something you're experiencing, then your marketing dollars are probably going to be diluted, and the consumer may mistakenly contact your company instead of the similarly named one or vice versa.

- **Is the name trademarked?** This is an important consideration, especially if you plan to have your brand in multiple states. We've seen many issues arise from companies that start their business with a name that is already trademarked. They invest so much into that branding, only to learn later on that the name is trademarked by another company. You see this mistake made often, when companies only perform a search of their state's business registry and believe that if no one in their state is using that name, they're free to use it. Unfortunately, that's not the case. Federal trademarks supersede that of states, so even if your name is technically available in your state, it doesn't mean you can use it now and not be served a cease-and-desist letter later. We've seen this happen in many instances, especially from private equity firms exercising their intellectual property rights as they plan expansions in other markets. The best advice is to consult an attorney when you've narrowed down your name to be sure it's a name you can use. We discuss this in detail in chapter 12.

- **Is the name overly aggressive in nature or overtly masculine?** Always keep in mind who your brand name is meant to attract, and be mindful of names that suggest an aggressive or somewhat threatening notion. Your goal is to put the homeowner at ease and make them feel comfortable with who is about to show up at their house and provide service. Don't use names that may add to that apprehension. For example, Viper Air Conditioning doesn't sound nearly as welcoming as Comfort Heroes does. In most instances, women remain the key demographic you are trying to attract with your branding. Make sure the name feels welcoming to them, and you'll be starting on the right foot.

- **Does the name make an easy target?** Some names make it easy for a competitor to build a campaign against you, whether it's subtle or direct. Sometimes the name itself— even without a competitor trying to use it against you— doesn't make much sense to the homeowner because it already sounds like something to perhaps be afraid of (as noted above). For example, a few years ago, Scorpion, which was a competitor of ours in web design, bought every branded search term for our company name. So any searches for KickCharge™ would show their paid ad above our listing. It was kind of flattering at the time, as I don't really consider us to be competitors at all, but they thought highly enough of us to buy our branded keywords. Consider how easy it might have been to counter their ads with our own, using a headline such as: "Don't get stung by your marketing company." The name made it simple to counter their advertising if we had chosen to (we didn't, however).

Don't make it easy for people to launch attacks with a name that may already have a negative connotation. You wouldn't name your company Snake Heating and Air, right? It would be way too easy for a competitor to capitalize on that, and it would obviously make the homeowner, who's already worried about getting ripped off, feel very uneasy.

- **Does the name attract the wrong customer?** Avoid names that include words like "Budget," "Value," or "Affordable," as they make it almost impossible for you to be viewed as anything other than cheap. If you wanted to get higher average tickets, you'd have a homeowner who's not happy that you're charging as much as you are. We've rebranded several companies with names like these examples, and the results have been amazing. These companies have been able to charge more for their services and find the right type of customer who is willing to pay for a premium home service experience.

- **Does the name use vague terminology or industry jargon?** It seems like, for a time, it was all the rage for home service companies to add the phrase "home service" as they added new lines of business. For example, a company that started as HVAC only and later added plumbing would suddenly go from Smith Heating and Air to Smith Home Service. Seems like that would make sense, right? Because now they're covered as they add services, like electrical or solar, down the road. Makes sense until you realize that "home service" as a brand clarifier clarifies nothing at all. Homeowners don't automatically equate "home service" with their mechanical systems. In fact, many believe "home service" to mean anything at all related to the home, such as roofing, siding, kitchens, or landscaping. After all, those are all home services. So because your brand clarifier clarifies nothing, then all your advertising needs to clarify the home service you offer. At that point, what is the point of such a vague clarifier? While we have branded many companies who wanted to keep "home service" in their name, for others, we've either deleted it from their current name or reverted to just listing the services as brand clarifiers under their name. It makes the truck wraps so much cleaner, and there is no ambiguity about what they provide.

Worse than "home service" as a clarifier are names that use just "services" (such as DS Services) as their clarifier. It doesn't get any more meaningless to your customers than that. What services are we even talking about? Oh, I guess they'll need to read all the bullet points on your truck and elsewhere to even know what we do. It makes no sense at all, yet you see it all the time. Make it easy for people to know what you do; don't expect them to guess. Or just plan to spend more money on your advertising educating them.

Another poor clarifier is the word "solutions" if it's preceded by a word that does not state the nature of the service being provided. Names like TDS Solutions or Top-Notch Solutions tell us absolutely nothing about the service offered.

Lastly, names that use industry terms such as "HVAC" or "mechanical" should also be avoided. Most homeowners have no idea what either term means. In fact, there is even more confusion from homeowners about the term "mechanical" because they relate it to automotive services. (If you're doing a lot of commercial work, then those names are probably fine, since your target audience would understand those terms.)

- **Does the name only mean something to you?** Some people start their business with a name that holds a deep, spiritual meaning to themselves. But the average person has no idea why your home service is called what it is and how that company will solve their problem. Often, you'll hear owners talk about "everyone asks me what it means"—as if that is some kind of validation of why it's a great name. For every person who asks you what it means, there are 100 who could not care less about it and won't ever bother to find out.

- **How does the name make people feel?** Great names make people feel something about your business. Whether it's humorous, nostalgic, or fun, if your name can help create a connection, it's far more likely to be remembered.

- **Does the name include "Inc." or "LLC"?** Although this is not as big an issue as a poor name in general, adding "LLC" or "Inc." to your name in your logo is not necessary and looks amateurish. Fire the attorney who said you need to have it in your logo, as they are incorrect. Did you ever wonder why companies like Apple, Nike, and McDonald's don't have "Inc." or "LLC" in their logos? Did they somehow secure special permission from the governing body of all things logo? Logos are not legal representations of anything. Your contracts should include the full legal name of your company (generally just typed above your address), but you never need to use "Inc." or "LLC" in your logo. With over 2,000 logos under our belt, we've never had a single instance of using "Inc." or "LLC" in any logo thus far, and no one has been sued.

## Brand promise in naming.

If you want to rename your business, one approach is to look for a name that infers a brand promise: a name that, when taken by itself, leads the consumer to believe something about your company that delivers a positive expectation. The idea is to control their perception of the company before they experience your service. So names like **Air Experts**, **Comfort Cavalry**, **On the Mark**, **Bee Right There**, **Blue Ribbon**, and **Over the Moon** all speak to a positive expectation of some type of deliverable—whether it might be expertise, comfort, precision, or timeliness.

You should also consider a name that speaks to the solution to a specific problem a homeowner may have, and how you can solve it. **On Time Experts Heating and Air** speaks to the idea of timeliness right in their name. They'll be there on time for you. This speaks to an inherent challenge homeowners face when trying to schedule work at their home. They want to know when you're arriving. This name's brand promise speaks directly to one of their concerns (timeliness) while simultaneously speaking to expertise. So not only will they show up on time, they are experts at their craft.

The majority of existing brand names within the service industry are either neutral, with no brand promise inferred, or they're negative. The most common neutral brand names are last-name-based brands and names with initials. Over time and with a lot of advertising, you can get a last-name brand to gain a brand promise. Brand names like **Goettl** have developed a brand promise over time, with repeated, consistent advertising that hammers their brand story. However, were you to start a new brand today, it makes little sense to use your last name. It will take too long for people to associate your brand with a specific brand promise.

# Brand controls the consumer's first impression. Service controls the last impression.

It's much easier to start with a name people already associate with what your company stands for and can deliver. Remember, so much of what branding is meant to do is control initial impressions. Once you're inside the house, of course you can wow the homeowner with great service. But we're most interested in what happens before. For brands based on a last name or initials, the process of the homeowner establishing your brand promise is largely happening after you ring the doorbell—not before. Unless, of course, you advertised heavily to have them learn what your brand promise is.

Brand controls the consumer's first impression. Service controls the last impression. The first impression gets you inside their home. The service you deliver is what they'll remember when you leave. The last impression is the lasting impression. That's the one that counts.

The ideal brand name gets the consumer to feel something about your brand. It makes emotional connections that lead them to believe the experience with your company will be superior to one without any brand promise inherent in their name. Lead with something positive, and you'll be way ahead of the competition already.

**Here are a few examples:**

- **Over the Moon.** Names like this already speak to the idea of how the customer will feel after you provide service to them.

- **Full Speed Plumbing.** This speaks to a common concern: How quickly can you get here? Full speed? Great! It also suggests your plumbing will also operate at full speed, meaning that your drains work correctly and efficiently.

- **Zen Air.** Everyone wants to be in a state of Zen in their homes. This name suggests how the homeowner will feel at ease and peaceful after your service call.

- **Bee Right There.** Yet another name that speaks to speed and appeals to the consumer's key concern about how quickly you can arrive and make their pain go away.

Chapter 5 talks more about consumer bias against contractors. Right now we'll focus on why it's important to choose a name that helps diffuse that bias and set up in the consumer's mind a positive expectation of your service and how you're different from other contractors. It goes a long way toward establishing a great foundation for a positive first impression. Who would you rather do business with if all things were equal: Over the Moon Heating and Air or CK Mechanical? This is literally how consumers think about home service brands when they make decisions about who to call, who to trust, and to whom they award the job.

## Consider names that conjure up specific visuals.

Some of the most well-known brands are almost pictographs of their name. Take Apple, for example, whose logo is—wait for it—an apple! Well, of course it is. The beauty of this naming strategy is that if you covered up the name and only looked at the symbol or graphic, you could almost guess the name of the company. Conversely, another beauty of this strategy is that if you simply say the name of the company, you already can imagine what the logo might even look like—without ever seeing it.

It's not often that these types of names exist in the home service industry, but imagine if you covered up your name and people could simply look at your mark or mascot and already know or guess the name of your company. Think of how much easier it would be for people to remember your company name at the time they need services with a simple, easy-to-remember name with a visual that is a pictograph of the name.

**Here are a few examples:**

- **Red Seal Plumbing**

- **Cardinal Heating and Air**

- **JackRabbit Air Conditioning**

- **All Heart Heating and Cooling**

- **Blue Ribbon Heating and Cooling**

You can see how the names above are almost literal pictographs of the brand name. As such, they are easy to remember at a glance, which is critical for the success of your outdoor advertising and fleet branding. The repetition of those impressions is largely what helps drive increases in organic branded search terms. Having the consumer remember your brand name is our primary goal and certainly the key to how we win on the streets with our wrap designs. No matter how good your SEO company is, the easiest way to the top of a search query is a branded search query.

Of course, it's also important to avoid obvious visuals with your name that you can't own due to their prevalence within an industry. If you're an HVAC company, avoid using clip-art approaches, such as red and blue arrows. If you're a plumber, avoid pipe wrenches. If you're a roofer, avoid roofs.

## Disruptive naming strategy.

Some of the most interesting names we've created for home service businesses don't sound like names for home service businesses. Wait—what? That doesn't make any sense, right? Shouldn't a name for a home service company sound like what you'd expect to be used for a home service company? Well, if it sounds like what you'd expect, then don't you run the risk of it sounding like every other home service company?

We talk so much about visual disruption as one of the hallmarks of a successful brand strategy, but disruptive names aim to do the same. They aim to be the verbal version of the purple cow. And what's great about them is when they are done right, you're able to build such a great and unique foundation for a truly disruptive brand.

The interesting thing about names like these is that most home service businesses are so afraid of them. Their natural instinct is to think like everyone else and go with common names that feel very safe to them. But being safe is just another way of being unremarkable. It does take some guts to once again zig when everyone else is zagging.

We generally pitch three or four names when we do naming for a client. We encourage clients to be careful about sharing the names with other people, as most people simply won't understand the mission, the story, and the "why" behind any of these names. It's only natural to want to share with people and get their opinions. But sometimes their feedback psyches out the clients—either because the people they share it with are also expecting this name to sound like all the other home service names they've heard of before or because they expect the name to basically fit that stereotypical mold of what they think a home service name should emulate. It's that exact feedback that essentially proves the point of why a disruptive name is a good idea.

When a client comes back and says, "I shared the name(s) with my friends and employees, and no one got it; they said it doesn't sound like an HVAC company," for me, that is all the validation I need. They've helped prove the name to be disruptive.

The problem is that many owners are afraid to go against the grain and instead opt for safe names. It takes a certain amount of guts to adopt this strategy, but in every instance, we've gone through, the results have yielded the highest returns. Just don't expect everyone to get it at first. Later, they'll say you're a genius—

but initially, they may think you're just plain crazy, and so is your agency for recommending it. It's okay. It wouldn't be the first time we were told that.

Wisconsin-based **In Phase Electric** is an example of a somewhat vague name, with no particular brand promise inferred and no specific visual to go with it. Most people don't know about the technicalities of electricity and what the word "phase" even means. It's jargon, to a certain extent. So what name did we come with instead? **Over the Moon**. You know, because a cow jumping over a moon that looks like cheese makes total sense for an electrical contractor. Just describing that probably sounds completely ridiculous. But that's exactly why it's genius.

Another startup we named with this strategy is **Turtley Awesome Cooling and Heating** in Florida. Of course, every homeowner wants their experience to be totally awesome, right? Their fun brand story, image, and wrap design has resonated well in their community. And the name is really hard to forget—especially after seeing their unique truck wrap design. We also wrote their tagline: "Awesome Service You Can Turtley Trust." The whole concept is intentionally disruptive, while still speaking to an amazing brand experience. Most of the client's friends said, "That doesn't sound like a normal heating and air conditioning company." Perfect! Because the minute it does, the harder it will be to remember compared to all the normal-sounding heating and air conditioning companies.

## The myth of "world-class" brand names.

Beware of names that sound like they're owned by some large corporate entity. Names that sound so large are challenging for consumers to connect to. Remember what we said earlier about brand story and creating empathy with your audience. When someone invites you into their home, they want to believe that there are real people and a connection to your community behind the brand name. So while you want to avoid "Joe's Heating and Air" because it sounds too small, you don't want to sound like "Emron" either. Somewhere in the middle typically works great.

# Duuuuuude. Our brand is Turtley Awesome.

A disruptive brand-name strategy is totally personified in the startup brand we created for **Turtley Awesome**.

"I have never in my 28 years in the industry had people taking pictures of my vehicles. I swear I've had a minimum of 12 to 15 people take pictures and come up to me and tell how awesome the van and truck look. People passing me on the freeway and rolling down the window giving me the surf's-up sign. People absolutely love it. We have had a 212% increase in revenue since the brand launch."
**—Michael King, President**

**CALL 321-710-5172 TODAY!** | 📅 BOOK NOW | 🗓 SCHEDULE NOW! | 📞 GET IN TOUCH

Awesome Service
· You Can ·
**TURTLEY TRUST!**

COOLING    HEATING    OTHER SERVICES    ABOUT US    RESOURCES    CONTACT

AWESOME SERVICE YOU CAN TURTLEY TRUST

## Turtley Awesome Cooling & Heating

Are your vents looking gnarly? Is oppressive humidity slowing you down to a crawl? Turtley Awesome HVAC technicians have got your back. Our steady service thrashes anything other AC companies in Melbourne, FL, can muster.

BOOK AN APPOINTMENT

SERVICES

## Reliable Home Care

Turtley Awesome technicians are committed to quality work every time. Our steady service ensures that your HVAC system delivers complete comfort on demand. But our technicians aren't just amazing at repairs and installations. We go out of our way to communicate our findings and recommendations to our clients so they won't be caught off guard by nasty surprises.

### AC REPAIR

Don't let a busted air conditioner leave you shellshocked in the middle of a Florida summer. The certified pros at Turtley Awesome can repair any make and model of air conditioner to restore your home to total comfort.

### MAINTENANCE PLAN

Customers who sign up for our Turtley Protected maintenance plans never have to shell out wads of cash for repairs. You'll receive two annual visits to keep your system in tip-top shape. If our Turtle techs discover something wrong, we provide priority service and repair discounts to get your AC running like new.

### DUCTLESS MINI-SPLIT

Ductless mini-splits offer the best of all worlds, providing great cooling and heating while keeping your energy bills low. Our team can advise you if your home is a good candidate for a unit. We're Turtley Awesome at installations, repairs and maintenance.

### DUCT CLEANING

With Florida's heat and humidity, you'll want to stay on top of cleaning your air ducts. Mold, mildew and critters can make themselves at home here, lowering the quality of your home's air.

WHY CHOOSE US

## We Stick Our Neck Out for Our Customers

Turtley Awesome pairs fantastic service with a great price point. Our small business offers financing, discounts and maintenance plans to help you keep up with needed repairs and upgrades. We're no amateurs, either. While our AC company is new to Melbourne, FL, we've accumulated more than 30 years of HVAC experience serving customers across the American South. We're ready to put our hard-earned knowledge and skills to good use in Brevard and Indian River counties. We bring new meaning to the phrase "shell corporation"—and, in our case, it's Turtley Awesome!

LEARN MORE

We'll talk more in detail about logos themselves, which deploy this characteristic, but it's safe to say that usually, the bigger the feel, the more impersonal the brand. It's one of the reasons why mascot-based brands perform so well. It's the opposite approach: They're warm and friendly as opposed to cold and impersonal.

Recently, an appliance repair company named **Felix Appliance** wanted to add HVAC to their services. They were advised to start a new company called **Golden Sword Services** instead of just adding that to Felix Appliance. That new name was confusing and even somewhat menacing to homeowners. Why would a sword be a comforting image or visual to someone who needed HVAC services? We recommended they abandon the new name and simply rebrand under **Felix Appliance • Heating • Air**, and they're doing so much better in their market now. It's a much friendlier brand, and it connects with women much better than Golden Sword.

## Alliteration and sticky names.

One simple technique used in developing sticky names is alliteration, which is the occurrence of the same letter or sound at the beginning of adjacent or closely connected words. This is a tried-and-true advertising technique. Think about some of the household brands you already know, like American Airlines, PayPal, and Range Rover.

Studies have proven that alliteration aids in memorization; thus, branded names that use alliteration are key in forming top-of-mind awareness. And with that top-of-mind awareness comes another key element to winning in digital marketing. Because now, consumers are searching for that sticky brand name online, and it's so much easier to be ranked higher for your brand than it is for "heating repair company Boise Idaho."

**Here are a few examples:**

- **Stepping Stones**
- **Comfort Cavalry**
- **Authentic Air**
- **Bumble Breeze**
- **Carpet Chemist**

## Made-up names.

One of the biggest challenges you may have in naming your home service business is finding a name that you can legally use that speaks to brand promise. With more and more names being trademarked in the home service classification, the ability to find a name that hasn't been thought of before or is not yet registered as someone's trademark is daunting. Perhaps that's why many startups give up and simply go with a last name, since that path is usually much easier. But there are other ways to go about this, and certainly using a made-up name or phrase is one way to go about it. There is a higher likelihood that you'll be able to trademark that name or phrase, and certainly, solely owning that unique name has benefits.

Of course, having a unique name that no one has thought of before all sounds great. But it's also really hard to do well.

In 2017 we renamed our agency KickCharge™. We felt that name captured us perfectly. It personifies what we, as an agency, do for our clients. We energize brands; we power them with smart marketing solutions. Our name can also be used as an adjective or a verb, as with "Get your brand KickCharged™" or "KickCharge™ your brand." This naming technique deploys a common concept of

putting two words together to form a single name. PayPal is a good example of not only alliteration but also this technique.

You can also create names that use unique spelling. However, be careful with names that are spelled differently than they sound, since it may impact your online searches or not work well when said aloud on radio or TV.

**Here are a few examples:**

- **Fetch-A-Tech.** For this name, we wanted to think a little outside the box and create a name that we could build a strong visual around, as well as one that would speak to the idea of getting a technician to show up at your house.

- **Hop2It.** Again, this made-up name lent itself to a specific visual to go along with it. The idea of speed as a USP is leveraged in a name like this.

- **Fixmatic.** This made-up name was used for an appliance repair company. We developed a retro-based brand around the name,

*Previously named 24/7 Electrical Services, this company struggled with organic branded searches and being sticky with their name. We renamed them Hop2It!, which gave us a great foundation to build a memorable brand image and craft story elements.*

which connects the name to the visuals. It not only sounds like an appliance repair company, but it looks like one.

- **Plumbs Up.** A playful take on the common phrase "thumbs-up" for a plumbing company in Canada. The visual of the hand giving a thumbs-up while holding a plunger connects the idea visually while delivering brand promise.

## Domain availability and social media handles.

The list of available branded dot-coms is certainly getting smaller and smaller each day, so it's often impossible to get the exact brand name with a dot-com. Although there are more widely available domains (.net, .biz), it's always preferable to get the dot-com. Sometimes, if the dot-com is not available, we'll suggest adding the word "call" in front of the brand name. Thus, the URL that is promoted is also something of a call to action for the homeowner.

Be sure to research the availability of social media handles to use with your brand name. Again, you may need to be creative if your name is taken.

## Keep it short.

Generally speaking, the shorter your name, the better. As a rule, try to keep your name to four or fewer consonants. Names with one consonant are tough to come by, but don't be afraid to think outside the box on very short names. There are logistical reasons why short names work very well when considering how they work for a logo. Quite simply, the shorter the word, the bigger it can be on your trucks and elsewhere. It's much easier to read from a distance and has more punch on your marketing.

Here are some examples of home service companies we've named that are succinct:

- **Zest Plumbing.** Zest isn't a name strongly associated with plumbing, but it does have a positive connotation, which suggests that this company approaches every job with energy and enthusiasm. The key was to connect the name with a visual and marry the ideas together. We also wrote the tagline

"Refreshingly Good Service" to relate to the name in a fun way while also speaking of the unique deliverable they provide. Their previous name was Affordable Plumbing Rooter, which was not only long but a limiting name that attracted customers who aren't willing to pay for a premium service. The previous truck wraps generated seven phone calls in an entire year, and within three months of rebranding, they had a total of 21 calls. That means they're on a pace of 84 calls for the year, or roughly a 12x increase. Revenue was up 79% in the second month of launching compared to the same month the year prior.

- **Dandy Painting.** "Dandy" is a fun word that we leveraged from the phrase "fine and dandy." "Dandy" means having done a good job as well as a man devoted to style, neatness, and fashion in dress and appearance. These are all positive concepts that we leveraged in the building of their brand imagery.

## Can last-name brands ever work?

Can you ever successfully use a last name for your brand name? Well, sure. Thousands do all the time. But if you were starting your company today, we definitely wouldn't recommend it. However, there are certain last names that you could brand better than other last names. The primary difference would be if the last name can be connected with a specific visual. That's the only instance where we would say a last-name brand could work. We've created many brands that were based on a last name that we could connect a unique and compelling visual to, and those companies have done very well. Of the many we have done, their prior branding had no visuals to connect their name with, and as such, they were not performing very well in the market.

**Here are some examples:**

- **Barker.** For this last-name brand, we connected the idea of a dog to go along with the name and developed the tagline "Your Companion for a Healthy Home" to complement the visuals of the dog. If you view the prior branding, you can see how it blended in, and there wasn't anything memorable about it to connect with the name.

- **Colepepper.** This was a tougher name to connect with an obvious visual. We chose to focus on the "pepper" part of the name and build a brand with a fun mascot based on an actual pepper. The results were dramatic compared to their prior brand, with over 80 phone calls attributed to the vehicles in the first six months of service versus zero in the six months prior.

- **Hartford.** This name doesn't conjure up a specific visual by itself, but maybe focusing on the "Hart" would translate into a visual. So we created a literal heart graphic made up of red and blue waves (to connect to heating air) and developed the tagline "We Put Our Heart into Service." In doing so, the name, visual, and tagline all connect and help tell the story.

## Self-limiting names.

While it's hard to completely future-proof your name, care should be taken to consider where you might see your business in the future. For example, if your business is currently only focused on heating and cooling and your name is specific to that trade, what would happen if you added a service to your business? If plumbing was added to your name, could you still use it? What signal would the name send to consumers, and would it be hard for them to believe you were good at this new additional trade? If your original name were "Awesome Electrical," would you be able to have people think you had expertise in heating and air if you added those services later? Use caution when labeling yourself with trade-specific terminology, as it may, in effect, pigeonhole you to that trade, making it hard to add another service later.

## Names that are generic.

Be careful with names that are so descriptive that they can't be owned as a branded search term. While they may say what you do, they make it hard for people to know who you are. A perfect example is a local company whose van I see often. It says "Handyman" in big letters with a bright red hammer. Okay, great. I can see you are a handyman. But how do I find you? Do I just google "handyman" and hope that the van I saw will magically show up in the search query? Always make sure your name has a unique component, or you're simply going to be lost in the mass of Google listings for companies fighting for the very same keywords.

## Names and company perception.

The name you take on will go a long way in helping determine that first impression of your business. This is not only important to the consumers you are trying to connect to but the employees as well. What signal or vibe does the name give off to them? Remember that before we rebranded and renamed, we were called Graphic D-Signs. It wasn't a good name to attract employees. After we renamed the agency KickCharge™, we had so much more interest in candidates wanting to work here. Even if all things before renaming were the same, it simply sounded like a cool place to work. If your name can appeal to both internal and external audiences, that's a huge plus.

*Rise & Shine was previously named Garage Door Repair Company, which was generic and difficult for consumers to remember. It also presented challenges online for branded searches, because the name sounded more like a search term than an actual brand name.*

## Naming checklist.

As you zero in on specific names, consider the points above, and narrow down your list to names that check off as many of the boxes below as possible.

- **Does it give a good first impression?**

- **Is it easy to spell?**

- **When spoken, would people know how to spell it?**

- **How would it sound when used as your social media voice?**

- **Can you secure a dot-com with your name or one that is reasonably close to it?**

- **Does it speak to a positive brand promise?**

- **Does it give the consumer a sense of what service your company does?**

- **Is it unique enough that it will easily show up for branded online searches?**

- **Can you legally protect the name with a trademark?**

- **Is the name available in your state?**

## Isn't it a huge hassle to change your company name?

It's really not as much of a hassle as you might think. In most instances for companies we've renamed, the new name is registered simply as a DBA of the original name. This means you don't have to file any new corporate paperwork or set up a new LLC or S-Corp. There is some paperwork you need to file with the state for DBA, as well as changing the name on your license. When it comes to Google and your reviews online, those reviews can be transferred to your new name, so you won't have to worry about losing them. Your Facebook page name can be changed easily as well, so you won't lose all your fans there. And the rollout of the new name to your customers can be handled quite effectively with direct mail, email, and social media. More details about the rollout of a new name and rebranding are covered in chapter 11.

Even much of the SEO work that was done on your old site can be transitioned to a new site and new domain name. You may lose some rankings temporarily, but as long as redirects are put in place, you should be able to maintain much of the original investment in SEO.

## Choose wisely.

There is certainly a lot to consider when naming your home service brand or renaming an existing one. Keep in mind the points made above, which all essentially speak to the key idea that names should be remarkable while delivering brand promise. That's the ultimate benchmark. Names that accomplish both will ultimately perform better over the long term, and of course, they'll require less money to market them.

As you consider names and narrow down your options, you may be tempted to ask for a lot of opinions from people. Feedback can be useful, but sometimes it's difficult to judge a name without additional context as it relates to not only how a brand story would be crafted with the name but also specific visuals that are being planned to accompany it. Some of the most successful brand names we developed almost never saw the light of day because only the name was shared, with no context. People didn't get it because there was nothing else to accompany the name to support the foundations of the story the brand name would tell.

## Taglines and the promise of your brand.

Taglines are important because they lay the foundation for part of your brand story and serve to further illustrate your company's USP. They also aid in making your brand more memorable and emphasizing your company's mission and can help clarify the primary line of business.

**Keys to consider when selecting a tagline:**

- **Highlight your business type if your name is vague.** When a company has a name that doesn't clearly define its product or service offerings (like ABC Services), the tagline should help deliver a clearer understanding of the business type. An obvious way to determine whether this should be stressed in your tagline is to ask someone if they know what your company does just by looking at the logo. An ideal brand should answer the question of what the company does, but not every brand does that effectively. For those whose brand does not expressly communicate the nature of their business, the tagline becomes extremely important. For home service brands with last names or initials, this becomes even more important.

- **Use a tagline to connect your visuals to your story.** I love it when we're able to create a fun or interesting graphic element in a logo and then add a tagline that connects all the dots of why we have that graphic and how it relates to the brand story.

- **Create a tagline that helps personify the value you bring to the table and further accentuates a USP.** Consider a tagline as a means of distinguishing your company from those that offer a similar service. Is there something in your tagline that communicates a difference, whether perceived or real? Is there a USP that you can leverage in a tagline to help you connect to that homeowner? Consider these examples:

  - **Fetch-A-Tech: "Service That's a Breed Apart."** Note how the tagline relates to the name as well as a unique, declarative statement. Contrast that tagline with one like "Guaranteed Quality." Yawn. Totally forgettable, with no brand promise infused in it.

  - **Colonial Plumbing: "Service That's Revolutionary."** This isn't your ordinary home service company—they provide something above and beyond what everyone does.

  - **JackRabbit Air Conditioning: "When It Comes to Comfort, We're All Ears."** Although this tagline is a little longer than we normally like, it does a nice job of relating to the name and mascot. It also explains that this is a company that listens to its customers.

- **Avoid hyperbole.** Beware of using common phrases that can't be verified, and avoid overused terms that are not unique to you. "Satisfaction Guaranteed" and "Honest, Fair Pricing" blend in and are therefore not remembered. Adding the year the company was founded with a tagline that says "Great Service Since 19xx" is also not unique and not likely to be remembered. However, if you can couple the year you started with something unique about it, that can work. McQuillan Brothers is the oldest plumbing company in Minnesota. To highlight that fact, we came up with the tagline "Minnesota's Original Since 1883."

- **Limit your tagline to five words or less.** Try to minimize the number of words in your tagline. The more succinct, the more likely it is to be remembered. It's not meant to be a full mission statement or a complete sentence. It should be something short, impactful, and memorable.

- **Consider using alliteration.** Just as alliteration in your company name aids in brand recognition, it is also effective for taglines. Some examples might be "The Choice for Custom Cabinets" or "Time-Tested Technology."

*Formerly named Orange County Painting, we renamed them Rock & Rollers, and wrote a fun tagline, along with a memorable mascot and truck wrap design. Obviously, a thematic name and image goes a long was to standing out in a crowded market.*

- **Trademark your tagline.** Once you've established a tagline, it's a good idea to trademark it. Your tagline is an important brand asset, and trademarking it protects it from competitor use. While the process is not difficult, I would recommend going through an attorney who specializes in trademark registrations so that you can be sure it's done correctly.

Imagine a homeowner choosing between two same-name landscape companies with two different taglines: One company is "Prestige Landscaping: Builders of Exquisite Outdoor Environments," and the other is "Prestige Landscaping: Landscape Design & Construction." Which company sounds like it will build an amazing patio? Obviously, consumer purchasing decisions aren't based on a single tagline, but the tag helps to set the stage for a perceived brand experience. Of the two options, one also sounds more expensive. What if both companies provided the same estimate? One company sounds like a premium brand, and we might expect the consumer to choose that premium brand.

## Integration of your tagline into the branding.

The tagline does not always need to be positioned as a design element with the logo. Often, it is a separate design element that is used somewhere other than the brand architecture. For example, on a two-sided business card, it might be placed on the back with the company icon. On stationery, it might appear on the bottom as a design element. On a website, it might be deployed in the homepage animation sequence or in the footer.

If the company name doesn't explicitly communicate the business type, it becomes important to have the logo and tagline conjoined in a more obvious way. In these scenarios, the tagline aids in a greater understanding of the brand message.

# CHAPTER 5

# BRANDING AND THE HOME CONSUMER

# Branding and consumer bias.

Consumers have a fair amount of negative bias against contractors in general. They're afraid of who's coming to their house. They're afraid of being ripped off. They've seen too many news segments showing unscrupulous business practices where contractors have taken advantage of the homeowner. So they approach contractors with a lot of skepticism and concern. When they're told they need a new compressor, they wonder if it's really just a resistor gone bad instead.

While it's great to see the industry take major strides to help overcome some of this bias, it's still very real and something you need to concern yourself with. Your branding needs to speak to those concerns. It needs to make your potential customers feel something positive about your company.

Keep in mind that all branding is designed to have a reaction or impression formed by what is being presented. In our case, we're essentially trying to take control of that conversation. We're trying to make that homeowner believe something about your company before you ring the doorbell. We're attempting to rid the consumer of the inherent bias they have.

If we can control that first impression and make them believe you are, in fact, different than their bias suggests, then we've taken a huge step toward closing the sale. Again, bear in mind that your competitors likely do not have a handle on having their brands deliver a positive brand promise. Quite simply, the better the brand, the better your chances of closing the sale. There are so many home service sales coaches who will confirm this. When they deploy their sales training with well-branded companies, they see the best results—higher tickets, higher close ratios, and consumers who are more likely to believe the company provides value above its competitors.

This remains the biggest irony of many of the larger home service companies with poor brands. If only they leveraged a better brand, they'd grow so much faster. Bias is a real thing; ignore it at your peril or the peril of your close rate! As we discussed earlier, the fact that most larger home service companies are poorly branded and poorly positioned to counter the bias represents an opportunity for you to capitalize on.

## Branding and the home consumer.

The most important audience to keep in mind when building a home service brand is the homeowner. Understanding what appeals to them is a primary objective when considering the direction your branding should take. Contrary to what many company owners believe, the most important audience for their brand is not themselves. That's why decisions made about branding must be done from the vantage point of the homeowner and your ideal demographic.

Of course, from an agency perspective, we do want you to like your branding. But we're most concerned with trying to connect with that audience who's been conditioned to ignore you. How do we reach them, help them remember you, and encourage them to take action when they need your service?

## First, what does your ideal avatar look like?

Your branding should speak to who you identify as the ideal target consumer of your services. Think about the demographics of who typically calls your company. Are they women or men? How old are they? What does the typical household look like? How many people are in the family? Is it a dual-income household, or does one parent stay home? Do they care a lot about the environment? How old are they? Are they retired? Where do they live? Do they have pets?

Of course, there will be a mix of demographics for most home service companies. But try to think about the ideal customer—the one you want to have more of. Then tailor your branding and your advertising to communicate to that ideal audience.

Be cognizant of changing demographics and buyer habits as well. The 25- to 30-year-olds of today are going to be your customers of tomorrow. Making sure your brand is as future-proof as possible will help give your brand longevity.

For home service businesses, the vast majority of their customers making the initial contact with the company are women. This should be a huge consideration when looking at what approach your brand takes to connect with them. How can you make them feel at ease? How does your branding help them feel comfortable with who is coming to their home? How do you craft messaging that connects with the lady of the house on a deeper level and instills the trust you want them to have in your services?

## Exclusivity and higher average tickets.

Imagine that your brand offered this simple promise: Your brand is the choice of discerning homeowners who truly care about their families. If homeowners in your market thought that about your company, then pricing becomes a secondary concern— because they only want the best for their families. I'm sure you may have worked with homeowners like this who are willing to pay a premium for a premium service. While they want to be treated fairly, they are also not looking to find the cheapest company to take care of themselves and their families. That's exactly who your branding should be targeting: discerning customers who want the best. They also understand that the investment they are making needs to feel secure. So they'll pay a premium because they know if something goes wrong with their system, you will be around to service it and honor the warranty your company is providing. And of course, why would they also sign up for your maintenance plan? Same reasons. Because you look the part.

Think about your own buying habits and what you're willing to pay a premium for. Why would you pay more for a Porsche when a Toyota Corolla would also get you from point A to point B? Or a MacBook versus a PC? An iPhone versus Android? You'll pay a premium for a premium brand experience, the same way you'll pay $6 for Starbucks versus $1 for Folgers. You assign a higher expectation to those brands based on experience and, to a certain extent, the advertising that makes you feel they are premium.

This is one of the reasons why you need to be cautious about your advertising and what it communicates. Low-brow humor (e.g., "Your wife is hot; call XYZ Heating and Air") does not communicate premium brand experience. Therefore, you may encounter resistance if your tickets are higher than your competitors'.

The key for contractors is making the homeowner feel all those positive things about your brand and developing visuals and messaging that speak to that notion. Again, very few companies build brands that do this. Many of the largest home service companies fail to embody this idea. Thus, their ability to ask for higher tickets is often met with resistance because they haven't established a better sense in the minds of their customers as to why they should pay a premium for their service. I love that most of the larger home service companies are awful at embracing brand promise. Why? Because it represents an opportunity for my clients to exploit that shortcoming.

Keep in mind that even with the absolute best sales training for your sales team, if your branding is poor, it may be a really hard sell to convince a homeowner to spend more on your services than a competitor's.

## Make an emotional connection to your audience.

At the end of the day, people remember more information when it's associated with emotions and authentic feelings. This is one of the reasons why advertising that deploys pictures of condenser units really doesn't work well. The features of the condenser unit certainly don't specifically answer the question of how my life would be better if I had one. Does your brand help answer the question "How do you can make their pain go away?"

Consider the branding for Grasshopper Heating and Cooling, with the tagline "Forward Is a Way of Life™." Not only does this brand speak to the idea of moving your comfort forward, but it's also how they choose to do business. It's a powerful statement that certainly helps reinforce their "why" to their audience. Their growth has been exceptional. The brand and, of course, the great leadership that continues to reinforce their mission are huge components of their success. (See chapter 6 for more on their branding.)

We've seen great results creating brands that were based on a client's pet and building a memorable brand story around that visual. Again, we're trying to connect that homeowner to your business on a more personal level. Plus, many homeowners do have pets.

That's the irony of the "red and blue arrow syndrome" that afflicts so many HVAC brands. In addition to usually being awful-looking clip art, there is nothing about red and blue arrows to connect with homeowners on a personal level. And because it's such a common brand approach, there is little chance of them even remembering who you are, either.

*A huge mascot, disruptive colors, and a tagline that speaks to the heart of what homeowners fear about contractors help connect this brand to the consumer. Revenue grew by 77% in the two years after rebranding.*

## Humor sells, too.

Much like making an emotional connection, humor is also a way to brand your business while still being professional. We've deployed humorous approaches to many home service brands, and they always have performed exceptionally well—especially in comparison to some of their competitors' humorless and staid brands. It gives the homeowners something to smile about, and it shows that your brand is human, not some monolithic entity that they'd never be able to relate to on a personal level. The concept of humor in home service branding is not very popular, which by itself gives us a leg up on the idea of brand disruption. As long as the brand implementation and execution is done well, it can still be perceived to be professional.

The branding we did for Buehler Air plays off the humor of the last name, which is of course associated with the movie *Ferris Bueller's Day Off*. When we were asked to rebrand this company, it was previously called Air Source America, which is one of those names that no one could remember, or worse, it was confused with a company that provided oxygen. So we built a brand around a mascot that featured only the head of a guy with his sunglasses on. The tagline, "Stay Cooler with Buehler," was integrated into both print and radio. In a short time, the business became so top-of-mind in its market in Jacksonville, Florida. As noted earlier, it grew from $2.5 million to over $10 million in less than 36 months. And the beauty of the growth was that it happened with the company spending less than 4% of revenue on advertising.

Beware of humor that makes the homeowner wonder if you can be professional. That famous pickup truck that makes the driver look like he's sitting on a toilet probably generated a lot of funny looks, but I'm not quite sure the average ticket prices climbed much with that approach. I also doubt many potential employees were keen on the idea on driving that truck, either. So, just tread carefully should you endeavor to go in that direction, and make sure the humor doesn't come at the expense of professionalism.

## Become top-of-mind with your vehicle.

The easiest and most cost-effective way to become top-of-mind for homeowners is through your vehicles. Truck wrapping offers the lowest cost per impression compared to any other advertising vehicle. Awesome, right? Well, it is only awesome when it's executed correctly. But the sad reality is that most are not done correctly or done in a way that will help with top-of-mind awareness. Many wraps are a hot mess with too much information and poor brand integration. They're not memorable, and they certainly don't help deliver a brand promise. Most are those black and white cows blending into the countryside.

And if your truck isn't wrapped, then it probably suffers from the dreaded White Van Syndrome. That's when your truck is just another white van in the neighborhood, with essentially no chance of the homeowner paying any attention to it—let alone ever remembering it. (Chapter 7 goes into more detail on building an effective wrap design.)

Every time a homeowner sees your vehicle in their neighborhood or parked at a neighbor's house, an impression is formed. They are making assessments about your company whether you like it or

*Unique truck wraps like this generate far more attention than plain white vehicles. They also deliver a positive brand promise. We renamed this company (formerly called Antioch Heating and Air), and they had a 161% increase in revenue within six months.*

not. One of those assessments might be to completely forget about you because you've given them no reason to give you a second thought. Or maybe they do see your vehicles—perhaps many of them—and they're all delivering a neutral or negative brand promise instead of a positive brand promise. In that case, your vehicles may be working against you and your mission to gain positive, top-of-mind awareness.

The more vehicles you own, the better your opportunity is to leverage those impressions. This is why sometimes a bigger fleet, although initially more expensive to rebrand, will achieve quicker brand awareness in your marketplace due to the saturation of a more disruptive brand and wrap design. We've found that a bigger fleet leads to increased awareness, more leads, and higher revenue.

When we were asked to create the branding for Gem Plumbing, Heating, Cooling & Electric in New England (a $100+ million company), the president wanted a wrap design that he termed an "aisle violator." I had never heard that phrase before. Basically, it's a type of signage in a supermarket that is meant to be viewed from both sides and essentially disrupts the shopper into viewing the advertising. As it relates to truck wraps, it's a great explanation of what you hope your truck will do.

# When they say branding is expensive, consider how expensive poor branding is for so many home service companies.

You want to violate the viewer's normal flow or train of thought. When we saw their prior truck wraps, clearly there was no aisle violation going on. The trucks simply blended in. Now, we had an owner of a huge home service company who wasn't complacent in the current branding, looking to make not just a small change, but a completely reimagined brand. For me, it was quite refreshing, as that openness and self-awareness are not prevalent in larger home service companies that are quite complacent. And the results were amazing: The company enjoyed four times the revenue attributed to their new branded truck wraps in one year with only 25% of the fleet rewrapped. That translates to 16x revenue with the full fleet rewrapped. When they say branding is expensive, consider how expensive poor branding is for so many home service companies.

Additionally, when done correctly, the vehicles themselves will help your online efforts by increasing the number of branded searches for your company name. This is one of the biggest benefits of the disruptive brand strategy. It's much easier for you to show up as #1 on Google for your own branded name than hoping to be #1 for "heating repair Union New Jersey." So while the online space is littered with competitors all fighting tooth and nail to get top rankings for unbranded terms, most are not fighting nearly as hard as they should be out on the street for that same top-of-mind awareness. Fun fact: SEO and PPC will never make your brand a household name.

Like the aisle violators in the supermarket and all the packaging that assaults the shopper, your trucks have a singular purpose to build your brand in your community and to disrupt consumers' normal psyche. The good news is that it's not that difficult to do with such a prevalence of poorly designed wraps and advertising assaulting them daily. The bad news is that without a solid brand, you're never going to be able to design a truly disruptive truck wrap. But more on that later.

## Make your visuals appealing to your audience.

As you consider various brand approaches, always keep the needs of homeowners in mind, especially women. Think about how your visuals will connect with them and help deliver that brand promise while countering any bias they may have. Again, we're trying to have them believe something about your company and service before you arrive at their home.

Of course, we're hoping the brand name does some of that work. But what about the visuals that represent the brand? Do they address the inherent worry about who will be working inside their home? Quite often, especially in mascot branding, the visuals are at odds with addressing their fears. Big, muscled superheroes carrying tools that can also be perceived as weapons are not exactly generating the warm and fuzzy approach that Mrs. Smith would like to see. So instead of a capable, competent technician arriving, you have someone who looks like if you don't pay their prices, you may be met with a physical assault. This isn't exactly the feeling that is going to help you build trust for that homeowner, especially women.

Contrast that aggressive approach with the feeling that one gets with the branding from Haven Air Conditioning. Who is more likely to arrive at my home to install a great system to keep my family safe and also truly cares about our comfort? And who might not beat the hell out of me if I question something about the install?

Does that thought process feel far-fetched for that homeowner? Remember, someone is coming to their home. They don't know if they need a new transistor or an entirely new unit. They've heard that there are unethical contractors selling things they might not need. And the logo seems very aggressive.

*This dude is coming to beat the piss out of you if you don't pay your bill. Not exactly that warm, fuzzy feeling that puts most homeowners at ease.*

*This much more peaceful, non-threatening, warm approach certainly connects better with women. Who would you rather have show up at your house?*

This exact thought process happens all the time. Are companies successful with aggressive names and visuals? Sure they are. But they're constantly going up against it. Perhaps after they've serviced the home a few times, trust is established. But what about the people who have never used their service before? First impressions are everything, and the wrong first impression (the truck on the street) may mean you never get a chance for the second one. So think carefully about what emotions your brand may evoke and what story it may tell.

## Be succinct in your brand.

Branding that delivers messages succinctly will always be preferable over branding that requires additional advertising to support the messaging. Most contractors do not have a huge budget to help explain their branding and get their story to the masses. As such, we believe it's far more important to develop brands that by themselves do a lot of that heavy lifting, so to speak.

Take your truck wrap, for example. Can you look at it by itself and learn much from it? Does it speak to the audience you are trying to attract and help them feel something about the experience they might get? Or is it vague and seemingly leaving the viewer with questions about your company—or, worse, what you do?

Therein lies the primary difference between corporate branding versus small business branding. Small businesses usually don't have the luxury of expensive media campaigns to help them understand who they are and what they do. It's the same reason why a Nike-like swoosh for your HVAC company would be a bad idea. No one is ever going to understand what that meaningless symbol is or what it's associated with unless you spend a serious amount of advertising dollars.

Wouldn't it be easier to use simple visuals that tell the gist of your brand story instead?

## Pitch to yourself.

As you consider your branding, it is easy to get caught up in whether you personally like it. Here's a fun fact: *It's not that important if you like it or not. What is really important is if the people you are trying to sell to—that ideal avatar—like it.* So pretend to be them. Examine your branding and be objective. Do all your marketing touchpoints speak to premium branding? Or are they a disjointed group of promotions, none of which have continuity or speak at all to the brand promise? If you were the consumer, would you want to pay more for the service? Or would you think that this company is going to be cheap or should be cheap?

Don't make the mistake of falling in love with your own branding despite all evidence suggesting that it's not working. We get it— it's like your own baby that you've nurtured for so long. But guess what? Babies grow up. They mature; they evolve. You remember them as they were young and what you got started with.

# Make them believe something positive about your company before you get there.

## Control the conversation.

All these points speak to one crucial objective for your branding: to control the conversation as best you can. **Make them believe something positive about your company before you get there— and then once you're inside the house, blow them away with amazing service.** When you do that, they'll become super fans, simply because you managed to live up to their expectations. And here's the cool part: Their expectations are the sum of all the impressions they've received about your company from all your channels. You set the expectations they have by how you present your business to them. That's how you kill it.

## Public relations.

Smart home service companies also have learned to leverage the power of good publicity and how that helps shape the conversations being held about a company. They let those impressions connect them to the community in a way that no other advertising really can. This type of exposure is invaluable when it comes to shaping the thoughts consumers have about your brand. I asked Heather Ripley, CEO and founder of Ripley PR, to speak about her experience in how home service companies can leverage PR as part of their overall brand strategy.

# The Power of PR

*Heather Ripley, CEO and founder of Ripley PR and author of* Next Level Now: PR Secrets to Drive Explosive Growth for your Home Service Business

Marketing is no mystery for savvy home service business owners. They understand that marketing and advertising are critical to making the phone ring. What many don't know is that to truly stand out from their competition, they need to do more. They need to position themselves as the credible expert in their market and in their industry. They need to push the envelope. That means going beyond using door hangers, radio or TV advertisements, amazing truck wraps, and other marketing services. And the only way to go that extra mile is through leveraging the power of public relations.

## Learning the business of public relations.

I have worked in public relations helping home service businesses for nearly 14 years. Supporting the skilled trades remains our focus at Ripley PR. I began representing home service businesses when I managed public relations for Clockwork Home Services and its three franchise brands, One Hour Heating & Air Conditioning, Benjamin Franklin Plumbing, and Mister Sparky.

It was at Clockwork that I first saw the real power of public relations for contractors. In 2009 I secured a spot on *The Celebrity Apprentice* that featured all of Clockwork's brands. This national promotion allowed Clockwork's CEO, Jim Abrams, the ability to sell the business for more than $180 million shortly after this appearance.

Home service public relations has been my passion ever since. I never forgot the time I spent at Clockwork Home Services even during my other endeavors. When I first thought about starting my own business, it was my experience at Clockwork that I drew upon. It opened my eyes to the fact that the home service industry needed to understand more about public relations. Earned media can help service businesses grow in ways that paid media cannot.

At my agency, we get to know our clients' needs and help them earn media coverage and promote brand awareness by positioning them as the local experts in their markets. We are intentional about the clients we work with and selective with the businesses we help, but we have grown steadily and comfortably since our inception in 2013.

## The differences between marketing, advertising, branding, and public relations.

While marketing, advertising, branding, and public relations are all closely related, they each bring their own dish to the family potluck dinner. You can have a decent meal if only marketing and advertising show up, but the dinner is much tastier and more satisfying if branding and public relations add their dishes as well.

Marketing, simply put, is all the messaging that your company puts out to the general public about itself. It is usually the overall budget under which the other disciplines are funded. Good marketers incorporate all these tactics and will research and evaluate which advertising channels and platforms will offer the best return on investment.

Advertising is the avenue that marketing uses to deliver its message. For home service businesses, advertising usually consists of radio and TV spots, truck wraps, billboards, direct mail, door hangers, and other paid media like newspaper and circular advertisements.

Branding is a cousin to advertising and marketing in that it is generally a part of the message that is being delivered via a marketing or ad campaign. **A home service company's brand is not just an easily recognizable logo on truck wraps, on the website, and in advertising; it's also what the company stands for and how it is perceived in the community.** A home service brand should immediately communicate something positive to the viewer, such as a commitment to work quality or community involvement.

Finally, and most importantly, is public relations. PR is the marketing tactic that very few home service businesses understand but is usually the best way to really stand apart from their competition.

Public relations builds mutually beneficial relationships by promoting your company's public image through positive earned media coverage in the news, in trade publications, and online through consumer reviews and posts. Earned media is coverage from a third-party journalist or reporter. If you've been interviewed by your local newspaper or featured in a trade publication, that's earned media. And research shows it's far more valuable to the consumer than paid advertising.

Most consumers don't trust advertising. They have become savvy to marketing strategies. But they do trust third-party endorsements. Most consumers say they trust what they read about a business when an independent authority reports on that business.

While advertising, marketing, and branding are essential, it's the relationships you build via public relations that can take your business to the next level.

## A strategy for the next level.

You've created a business plan. You've grown your business from two people and a van to 10 technicians. Now you're starting to think about your exit strategy down the road. How do you take your business from $2 million to $5 million? Or $5 million to $10 million? Or even $10 million to $20 million? How do you start winning awards or garnering speaking engagements that make your business attractive for acquisition or to make it stronger to pass to the next generation?

You can't do it by simply doing more of the same thing. Merely doing more marketing or more advertising isn't going to push you to the next level where you want to be.

Now you need an effective PR strategy that makes your brand visible to the right people and positions you as the expert in your field.

## Staying relevant.

One of the worst things you can do as a business owner is start a public relations project and then abandon it once you meet one or two goals.

You will need a strategy that includes a variety of ways to start new conversations about your business if you want to stay relevant and remain on the radar of journalists. Whether you are providing household tips, commenting on the news of the day, or promoting a charitable organization, you must keep telling your story to stay on the minds of consumers.

Another way to stay relevant is to keep an active and consistent message on social media networks and your blog. Posting a blog once in a blue moon or rarely engaging via your social media channels won't help you grow your business.

Public relations is the art of building relationships that last. Securing one opportunity with the media doesn't mean you should rest on your laurels. The opposite is true. One opportunity can be used to grow several more.

You should also handle yourself professionally and treat others as you would want to be treated. If you miss booked interviews with journalists or fail to return calls to media personalities who have done stories on you, you can get a reputation as being difficult or unreliable. When this happens, the media will write you off as uncooperative, and you may never get in that reporter's good graces again.

Remember that public relations is a marathon and not a sprint. Just because you don't see a tall tree the day after you plant an acorn, it doesn't mean that a tree will not grow.

## Why you should use a public relations agency.

Most business owners know they need to advertise, and they probably also know they need to do some marketing. They usually hire a dedicated marketer in-house to perform the specific functions of writing ad copy, planning events, and developing campaigns that bring in leads.

But just as you are the expert in your field, a public relations professional is an expert in theirs. While an in-house marketer is probably familiar with the concept of press releases and their functions, he or she may not know how to get a journalist interested in the release or what topics would make for an interesting story idea.

If a release crosses a journalist's desk and it's written in a promotional way or involves too much ad copy, that reporter is likely to throw it away or send it to the ad department to follow up on as paid advertising. You already have paid advertising. What you need is earned media.

PR agencies have the ability to think like a reporter, and that can help your business cut through roadblocks to secure earned media.

Public relations professionals are partners with your business. Not only do they know how to write the right copy and get it in front of the right journalists, but they also know how to work with you to provide ideas to tell your story. Many PR experts are former reporters or have spent their working life writing, creating content, and creatively developing story ideas or alternative avenues to get a story out.

By bringing in someone from the outside, you are also bringing in objectivity and dropping the blinders that an owner or employee may have. You and your employees have emotional attachments and financial investments that may prevent you from seeing how well a story idea will play with the general public.

## Picking the right partner.

Once you've decided to work with an outside public relations expert, you need to do your homework to find the right fit for your company. You might be tempted to hire a local public relations firm because they will happen to know your area market. An agency that knows the area is not as important as an agency that knows your business. A PR agency that has insider knowledge of the home service industry will be able to tailor a public relations strategy that better suits your business.

**Other qualities your PR partner should have include:**

- **A proven record of success.** Check with other home service businesses and see who has proven successful for them. Look for agencies that often have clients in the news.

- **Character and chemistry.** You have to work closely with your public relations agency, so you want someone you click with and who is well thought of both by other public relations professionals and by reporters.

- **The ability to tailor your public relations to your business.** Some PR agencies rely on cookie-cutter promotions and don't consider their clients' characteristics, needs, and goals. You want someone who listens to your ideas and develops plans to meet your goals.

- **Someone who can do an excellent job within your budget.** Look for a PR partner who wants to work with you to create a win-win relationship and is willing to take the time to explain the budget, the process, and the expectations.

Finally, your relationship with your PR agency isn't complete without input from the most important source: you.

Unless you are willing to embrace the relationship, listen to the experts, take chances, and share your hopes and aspirations, you won't get the most out of your partnership with your PR agency.

While they are the experts on how to get publicity for your business, they can't do it without your input. Tell them the events your company is involved in, tell them about your new hires, tell them about your growth, and keep them informed if your goals shift or your targets move. They may be professionals, but they are not mind readers.

Finally, public relations isn't just about garnering press and media attention. It's also about telling your story and building the relationships to continue to tell that story as your company grows and changes. PR is that fresh approach you have over your competitors. Doing it right will help you make that leap to the next level.

CHAPTER 6

# INTERNAL BRANDING

IRON MOUNTAIN PLUMBING™

435 383 3813

IRONMOUNTAINPLUMBING.COM

# What does your brand say?

Much of this book is focused on how brands work outwardly for the people to whom you are marketing. Clearly, that aspect can't be understated. However, your internal messaging is also important since it affects so much of your culture. It's how your brand story gets integrated within your organization and helps your team truly understand the mission and vision of your brand.

As brands send messages to homeowners you're trying to reach, they're also sending signals to the people already working for your company and those you're hoping to recruit as employees. Is there something unique about your message that will resonate with them? Is there something there that will make them care about your brand?

In many instances, there is not much being said. Too often what's being said is not at all aligned with the same outward brand story. Perhaps that's because so precious few even have a consistent brand story that can actually be defined.

## Goettl does things the right way, not the easy way.

In my view, no other home service brand in the country communicates brand story concepts externally and internally better than Goettl. Sure, I'm biased since it's probably the most successful home service brand we've created. But there are so many lessons to be learned about brand and culture from Goettl.

One only needs to tour their impressive Las Vegas facility to better understand this. The minute you walk in, you're greeted with consistent brand messages integrated throughout their workspace. The idea of doing things the right way, not the easy way is communicated visually through wall wraps in the space and, of course, through their extensive training facility. This notion is a top-down philosophy that is reinforced to everyone in the organization.

Think about how simple yet powerful that idea is to both audiences. To the consumer, it reinforces the idea of home service excellence. And to the people who work there, it's how all Goettl employees are expected to perform. It means the company is not interested in you taking shortcuts in the performance of your duties. The leadership expects you to do the right thing the right way for each task you perform.

Beyond the clever tagline for Goettl is the story of the boy holding the flashlight in their branding and what it's meant to communicate. When the brand was launched, a very successful ad campaign began that talked about the brand story behind the boy and the flashlight. The story revolved around the new owner, and how he used to hold a flashlight for his father as he worked on air conditioners. The ads had an emotional connection to those very homeowners they were trying to attract. It created empathy and helped them connect with the company.

At the same time, the story of the boy also connected with employees. The owner of Goettl started out as a technician—just like they did. That history certainly helps connect employees to management, who are better able to understand the challenges of employees because they cut their teeth in the trade as well.

For Goettl, I think the revenue numbers speak for themselves. When Goodrich acquired the company, they were hemorrhaging cash, and revenue was down to $7 million a year. They had a tarnished reputation in the community as well. Goodrich's first order of business was to rebrand the company. That decision, along with substantial infrastructure improvements, became the catalyst for significant change and was the start of an amazing turnaround. They grew to become the largest home service company in the U.S. with over $225 million in revenue in only eight years.

## Grasshoppers only move forward.

In early 2021, Amanda Triolo hired us to rename her company (previously named PMA Mechanical). I should note that changing the name wasn't what she asked us for initially. She wanted us to rebrand PMA Mechanical. We talked about the challenges with initial-based brand names and with having the word "mechanical" in the name (especially since she wanted to move more into residential sales).

We went through our normal process of ideating various names we thought would work for her and presented several options. But nothing connected with her. Then we thought more about her company's commitment to the community and to being conscious of environmental concerns.

I thought about some different names that could convey important aspects for the brand to communicate. Lo and behold, the name Grasshopper came to me. So I did a little research on grasshoppers. They are considered to be smart and beneficial to the environment, and there is an aspect of speed associated with them as well. I thought speed was a great brand promise to associate the brand with, since homeowners want their HVAC systems fixed fast.

But what I didn't know or even understand at the time was that grasshoppers can only move forward. Fortunately, Amanda knew about that special characteristic, and it became the foundation of their brand story. The business adopted "Forward Is a Way of Life™" as their tagline, which also became a powerful mantra for the company both externally and internally. It's the cornerstone of everything they believe in and reinforces their "why."

## Using wall wraps to reinforce your internal branding and culture.

Within your workspace, you have a great opportunity to reinforce your branding and remind employees of the mission and vision of the company. More than just using your brand colors throughout your space, think of ways critical messages can be regularly reinforced to the employees.

Training and conference rooms are great places to make use of your wall space and build a more visually stimulating environment. Wall wraps are a cost-effective way to reinforce some of your core values and help build a better culture and environment for your team. Here are some tips we've learned over the years in designing these spaces:

- **Feature real people and real photography when possible.** Branded photography is always going to be more impactful than stock photography. Showing real employees in uniform keeps the branding authentic.

- **Deploy your brand colors and various brand elements.** Don't just slap a logo on your wall. That's boring and certainly not inspiring. Instead, integrate the logo along with various brand assets.

- **Integrate core values and vision statements.** Remember to communicate your "why" to your employees. Help them understand that the mission is an important part of making sure everyone is truly on the same page. These types of graphics serve as a visual reminder of what the company's most important principles are.

- **Add history/timeline graphics.** For older companies, a timeline graphic can be a great way to help employees understand the company history and heritage and how you got where you are.

- **Consider word banks.** Word banks can be a fun way to reinforce your company's vibe. For our word bank, we asked each employee to give us a few words that they felt best described KickCharge™. You could do the same with your team.

- **Have fun!** Get creative with your wall wraps. Humor and creativity go a long way toward creating the right mood and vibe for your space.

*A sampling of some of the wall wraps we've created. When we built our new office, we got to integrate our branding not only into the wall wraps but into the flooring and furniture as well.*

# Forward Is a Way of Life™

*Amanda Triolo, CEO, Grasshopper Heating & Cooling*

In 2016 when I stepped into the HVAC world, commercial installation was the foundation of the company. Keeping the pipeline full was the goal to keep money flowing and guys moving. Here's what I learned over time: Being a small company in a large commercial world was going to equate to a sunken ship without a large amount of cash in the bank or an arsenal of skilled employees. I had neither the cash nor the people.

The marginal profit on the jobs was minimal to nonexistent, and I could not recruit or find a way to connect with people to grow this company as I pictured it in my head. I had a strong desire to lead people toward goals and growth but I saw no way of accomplishing this with the resources that I had. I am a believer in being relational in every way, and there was no proper pathway to relational with the road I was headed down. The company name was PMA Mechanical and all people cared about was what PMA stood for.

I essentially had nothing for people to believe in—to want to put their life and career in the hands of. At this point, I started diving into the research of the HVAC world as a whole. I saw very quickly that residential service had the ingredients to start the journey toward where I could see my company and that service was where the potential profitability was. I compared the high-stress work environments, low job margins, and slim pickings on the character of talent and suddenly envisioned that if I could only find a way to get into the residential world, these stresses and dead ends could

go away someday. I attempted for the better part of two to three years to pivot into residential. I could not find a way to do it without completely halting current business operations, bringing the bank account to running on fumes, and having no work or a slow start of picking up one job here and there to get moving. And then COVID hit. Within two weeks, the governor of New York closed down all construction job sites that we were working on.

I've learned you can do one of two things in life: You can sit back and let life happen to you, or you can stand up, fight, and find a way. Find a way forward...

We found a way forward. I immediately started connecting with other HVAC home service business owners throughout the United States and beyond. I noticed quickly that they had something in common; their branding was loud, awesome, incredibly modern, bold, and unforgettable. The pathway to these brands was Dan Antonelli at KickCharge™ Creative. I messaged Dan on social media in April 2020, just after a full month of the global pandemic essentially bringing the world as we knew it to a halt. Dan immediately let me know that my initial-based brand name needed to go. So did the word "mechanical" if my goal was to appeal to homeowners.

I took some time and made my final decision to move forward with a complete rebrand. While the world was shut down and there was no money coming in and no work in the pipeline, deciding to spend a good amount of money on a total rebrand was one of the scariest decisions I have made.

Five months later, Grasshopper Heating & Cooling was born. I get asked a lot, "Why Grasshopper?" Here's why: Grasshoppers facilitate decomposition and regrowth within the ecosystem. Decomposition and regrowth are the very heart of this company. Additionally, grasshoppers have the ability to move forward only. Moving forward is not only what we do, but it is who we are as a company. *We immediately had a purpose and a brand, not just a company*.

On February 1, 2021, Grasshopper launched (vehicles, website, mailers, and more). We had six fully wrapped Grasshopper vans hit the streets all at once. We got so many calls after just one week of the vehicles on the road. We even had a competitor call and congratulate me, saying their heads were spinning on where the heck this Grasshopper company came from. They were impressed.

We had other companies' employees walking up to my team in supply houses and at gas stations with many questions as to this Grasshopper company and where we came from. Fast-forward the next 60 days, and employee candidates started walking into our doors for a job with zero employment ads up and running. Many of them stated that the brand intrigued them and they saw our vans everywhere.

The culture started to evolve on its own. I spoke about grasshoppers only moving in a forward direction... Our company tagline is "Forward Is a Way of Life™" and that is what we believe as a team, both internally and externally. It is more than just a motivational line; it is who we are. Inspiring people is where I find passion, and for me, as an owner, I cannot believe that I found my purpose within an HVAC company.

"Forward Is a Way of Life™" is on three sides of every vehicle we wrapped and put on the streets. My hope is that if you're sitting behind one of our vehicles at a red light, drive by one of our vehicles on the street, or see our van at your neighbor's, maybe, just maybe "Forward Is a Way of Life™" is what you needed to read that day. No matter what hard times people may be facing, maybe it helps them forge forward as I had done. Like I stated previously, you can sit back and let life happen to you, or you can stand up, fight, and find a way.

## It is a beautiful thing when passion meets purpose.

Moving forward in life equates to growth, goals, momentum, progress, advancement—the list goes on. We are *huge* on growth with our team. Life change happens to every employee who becomes a Grasshopper. We bring all of them back to our tagline. This in itself has established its own culture within our team that each and every Grasshopper stands by. We celebrate our wins loud and proud. Our vision statement is: "We create opportunities that change lives and lead people to make great decisions."

When we rebranded, I learned very quickly that the brand promise and energy of the brand needed to match the experience clients would get. We present options on every single call, every single time, and let our clients make their best informed decision. This was a game-changing switch for how we conducted business and ran each call. Opportunities became possible and so did *massive* growth. In our first full year as Grasshopper (February 2021–February 2022) we earned $4.2 million in residential business alone and grew to 16 vehicles. That was a 3,303% jump in year one.

Can you imagine if I did not take the chance and spend the little money that I had left when COVID hit to rebrand with KickCharge™? Can you imagine if I let the world circumstances just happen without doing anything about them and let bankruptcy become a reality?

There was a time when I dreamed of what it would look like to lead people, inspire people, motivate real life change, have the ability to change people's lives, and help them find purpose in life and in their career. Because of everything that Grasshopper is and stands for, my dreams are now a reality. Spend the time, dream about it, write your goals down, pursue avenues, take chances, expand your mindset outside the box, and watch what comes of it. Fast-forward to today, and Grasshopper shows no signs of taking the foot off of the pedal and is forming a team to focus on total growth mode to continually become even bigger and better. Check back with us in three years! "Forward Is a Way of Life™."

# CHAPTER 7

# LEVERAGING YOUR BRAND TO WIN ON THE STREETS

# The keys to effective wrap design.

If you examined most vehicle wrap designs on the road today, you'd think the concept of designing a simple, easy-to-read message was difficult to understand. It's really not, once you understand the fundamentals of vehicle branding. Far too many wraps on the road today sadly represent a missed opportunity for those home service businesses.

Remember the chart from chapter 3 that showed how few people knew the name of a company before searching online for a service? It essentially proves the point that most home service businesses are doing an awful job of branding their companies. In fact, Google's data suggests that only about 15% of home service companies are remembered. Imagine all your marketing efforts and your marketing spend—and at the end of that, maybe 15% of the people you are trying to sell your services to even know your name. Wow, that must really suck to hear how much of your spend is wasted being unremarkable—especially on the street.

With so many wraps missing the basic fundamentals of effective brand integration on these moving billboards, what does that mean for you?

Well, the fact that there are so many poorly branded trucks on the road is a great thing for those who develop a more effective wrap design that is truly disruptive. These disruptive wraps have a much better chance of standing out and being noticed. So they become the purple cows in your community. And they help make your overall marketing spend go even further.

In fact, your vehicles are perhaps the single most important part of your brand efforts and one of the most cost-effective. In fact, one of our clients, Buehler Air, was able to attribute $1 million in revenue in one year from just 18 wrapped trucks. If these wraps cost an average of $4,000 per truck and last five years, then his total advertising spend per year was $14,400. To sum that up, he spent about $14,400 in one year on fleet branding that generated $1 million in revenue. Not sure I can think of a more cost-effective way to advertise. Of course, the key to the campaign's ROI is that the wraps and brand were creative and well-executed.

The before-and-after results aren't just speculative, as the difference in ROI between a well-branded fleet and a poorly branded vehicle has been proven time and time again.

The software that home service businesses use today makes it so much easier to track inbound lead sources and benchmark the ROI of the newly wrapped vehicles versus the older ones. In some instances, we've seen upwards of 16 times the amount of revenue being attributed to a better-designed wrap versus the old one. So this isn't some pie-in-the-sky theory about how important your fleet is when wrapped.

## Why are most wraps ineffective?

The failure of most wraps today can be traced to many factors. As evidenced by the abundance of ineffective wrap design, there is a lack of education and understanding about the actual medium. In the past, the prerequisites for billboard painters and truck lettering artists were years of study and apprenticeships. Entering the sign trade is a bit easier today since the primary barrier to entry is simply acquiring the cash to buy a large-format digital printer—not years of actual graphic design study. So, while a sign or wrap company may be brilliant at installing wraps, they probably lack experience in the study of effective outdoor advertising.

As odd as it sounds, it's not just sign companies that are unskilled in building effective wrap design. Traditional graphic designers and even agencies are often surprisingly ill-equipped to design effective wraps. The role that distance legibility plays in building effective wrap designs is often overlooked, and the lack of experience in the physicality of the medium contributes to those deficiencies. While

# A narwhal kills it on the streets—and online, too.

"At first, we were afraid a narwhal might be too out-of-the-box but we're so glad we trusted Dan and his team at KickCharge™. Their instincts were spot on! Narwhals are more popular and beloved than we first realized. It's been a conversation starter for interactions with customers, neighbors, and even admiring folks at the gas station. On the road, people flag us down at traffic lights to ask about it and kids point us out to their parents. We're still amazed by the daily 'Wow!' reactions to our trucks.

"Previously, referrals came from neighbors who knew each other. The new wrapped trucks generate calls from unrelated neighbors who spotted our vans in their community. But what surprised us most was how the trucks impacted organic searches and leads online. Literally within a day of launching three wrapped trucks, our search traffic increased 10x. In 2021, we grew 34%—a $340,000 increase in revenue 100% attributed to the trucks, because we didn't change anything else about our marketing." —*Jack and Kiki Curtin, PerfecTemp, Delray Beach, FL*

250

**Search traffic immediately following launch of three wrapped trucks**

0

Jan 25    Feb 12    Mar 2    Mar 20    Apr 7

| | | |
|---|---|---|
| ✓ Listing on Search | | 2.25K views |
| ✓ Listing on Maps | | 2.82K |

your design may seem legible on the computer screen while it's being created, how it performs in the real world is the biggest challenge. It's also a medium that is overlooked in graphic design schools today.

## Is my logo the problem?

In defense of some sign companies and designers, if they are given a poorly designed logo to build a wrap design with, there is only so much they can do to create something that will be effective for the medium. So they do the best they can, without ever addressing the fundamental truth in effective wrap design: You can't design an effective wrap design without an effective brand.

I know what you're thinking: "Woah! Wait a minute. So you're saying that just because my logo isn't great, I can't get an effective wrap design done with it?"

Bingo. That's exactly what I'm saying. Remember how we talked about the logo being the foundation of your brand, and without a solid foundation, your wheel won't turn effectively? So your next question may be "How come no one told me this?"

That's a more complex question. Who do you expect to tell you this information? It sort of reminds me of a quote from the movie *Spaceballs*, when Mel Brooks' character's head is somehow reversed on his body and he looks down and exclaims, "Why didn't somebody tell me my ass was so big?"

> # "Because my logo isn't great, you're saying I can't get an effective wrap design done with it?"

Why would the wrap company tell you that they can't wrap your truck because your logo is poorly designed? Well, they wouldn't. They need the work. And you didn't ask for their opinion, either. So they do the best they can with your logo, create a wrap, cash your check, and move on with their lives. You love the wrap, of course, because it features the logo you love.

Maybe it's the wrap company that created the ineffective logo and wrap design or that awesome crowdsourced designer you hired. Obviously, they're probably not going to tell you.

This same scenario plays out in a lot of your marketing channels. Did your digital marketing company ever talk to you about your branding or lack thereof? Or did you hand them your logo and send them on their way? Imagine them saying, "Well, your logo sucks, so we can't do any of your digital marketing." Ha!

Shouldn't every marketing vendor who takes money from you to promote your business ask these questions or work with you to make sure your foundation is solid? Most don't. Most are happy to cash your check, even though they know better brands yield better ROI for their clients. That's not rocket science, but I guess you might not sell many websites by pointing out to your prospects that their branding should be fixed before endeavoring to promote it.

We're constantly asked to design wraps for companies we have not branded that have poor brands. In those cases, we simply explain the challenges of the existing brand and discuss why rebranding would be beneficial. We also explain why the work they love on our site will never look anything like that with their brand. If they're not interested in rebranding, we completely understand, but we won't take on the job at that point. We're simply not going to be responsible for producing work that is destined to not deliver an effective ROI. Doing so would run contrary to our core values. We can't have your back if we're tasked with producing work that is not in your best interests.

## But everyone says they see my truck all over!

Cool story, my friend! I'm sure they do. But don't make the mistake of equating visibility with also delivering brand promise. That's where most home service businesses get it wrong. You could make your truck bright pink and people would say they see your trucks "all the time" as well. The key is to be seen while also delivering brand promise. That is the benchmark by which to measure the effectiveness of your truck wraps. What does your truck say about your company, and how does it connect to the consumer and make them feel something positive about the experience your company will provide?

There are many big companies out there that operate under the mistaken premise that being seen is the correct benchmark to assess the effectiveness of their weak brands and wrap designs. It's too bad for them that they don't get it and that they continue to overspend in other areas of their marketing to make up for their brand deficiencies. But their complacency is your opportunity. By being disruptive and delivering brand promise, your vehicles will deliver a far better ROI than theirs can ever hope to achieve.

## What about manufacturer logos and images on my truck wraps?

In theory, the cost-benefit of using the free marketing co-op dollars from your dealer if you include their logo on your truck sounds appealing. They promote their brand, and you get help funding the wraps for your brand. One problem with this is that you're promoting their brand at the expense of your own. Generally speaking, homeowners are less interested in the brand of systems you install and more interested in who is doing the installation and what their reputation is. Another problem is that the use of a manufacturer logo can suggest to the homeowner that you only service that one particular brand. Clearly, we don't want them to think that.

What we typically recommend is to use those co-op dollars elsewhere. Deploy a dedicated PPC campaign with a landing page that promotes that brand only or perhaps a direct mail campaign that features their equipment. Just don't use your truck for manufacturer logos.

## Truck wraps are brand-building tools. They are not meant to be a call to action.

Keep in mind that the primary objective of truck wraps is for brand building, not necessarily as a response mechanism or call to action.

Of course, you may happen to be driving next to someone who has just experienced an immediate need for your services, but it's more likely that the vast majority of people who come in contact with your branded trucks do not need service at that exact time. So the important thing is for your brand to become sticky in their minds so that when they do need service, they google your name instead of "air conditioning repair Jacksonville Florida." That's the real objective of a well-designed fleet of truck wraps: becoming top-of-mind to homeowners. This is one of the reasons why phone numbers are less relevant on the vehicle today. Think about the last time you dialed a phone number you saw on a truck. Consumers are more likely to google a company name and get the phone number that way or fill out a contact form.

This is why we don't like QR codes for vehicles. Outdoor advertising isn't really direct response. Its main purpose is for brand building.

## Research your market *before* you wrap your truck.

Before we design any brand and truck wrap for a client, we need to research their marketplace and examine which brands they compete against. We're typically looking at their top 10 competitors' brands, color schemes, and wraps. This allows us to decide which approach will create the most disruption in that particular market.

Are there too many mascots in this market? Then maybe we shouldn't add another. Are there too many red, white, and blue wraps? Then we're definitely not going to use red, white, and blue. Do any of the brands have a legitimate brand story that is unique and compelling? As we're designing, we have the images of these competitors' wraps handy so we can make sure we contrast with their approaches. The objective of this exercise is to make sure we help create that purple cow in your market.

If you are doing this yourself, sometimes it's helpful to simply print out images of all your competitors' truck wraps and make note of their color schemes and the kind of brand approaches they deploy. Print them all out, and tape them to your bulletin board or wall. Then you can do a quick SWOT analysis of their trucks. A SWOT analysis is a strategic management technique that can help identify strengths, weaknesses, opportunities, and threats related to your competition or project planning.

Is there any semblance of a brand story your competitors are communicating? Do their taglines offer the consumer a compelling reason to choose them? Are there deficiencies in how their wraps are executed?

When we do this for the brands we create for our clients, it's often revealing and, sometimes, even surprising. Often, the biggest surprise in a market is just how awful the competition is at branding their companies and truck wraps. Although I'm familiar with the competition in many markets, it's still perplexing to see how often big companies give off the vibe of a one-truck operation by how their vehicles look. But again, their weakness is your opportunity to more easily disrupt your market. Their complacency can easily be exploited.

Don't forget to also review non-competitors in your market. Perhaps there is a fleet of trucks in a different industry that is very eye-catching and unique. We certainly don't want your vans to be mistaken for theirs.

The following rules can help you better understand the fundamentals of designing an effective vehicle wrap. Whether you are a designer hoping to improve your layouts or a small business owner trying to gain market share, these fleet branding ideas will help you make the most impact and get the maximum ROI for your outdoor vehicle advertising programs.

## Rule #1: Start with a great brand.

Your brand should always be the primary message for a vehicle wrap, unless you have national brand recognition. For home service businesses trying to make an impact in their communities, the message is always about the brand. Starting with a poor brand means you've failed before you've begun—by wasting money on a wrap and missing a huge marketing opportunity.

The brand is the message, period. Marginal brands will always yield marginal results.

## Rule #2: Don't use photos.

Few creative truck wraps that use photos are effective, and I'd argue that any wrap that uses a photo could have been designed more effectively without one. A photo is not a brand identity; it doesn't connect the audience with the business name. Maybe it tells the viewer what the company does, but so should a good brand.

Take a typical HVAC contractor with a picture of an air conditioner on their truck. Great. Now I may understand that your company fixes air conditioners, but I still don't know who you are, because I only have 2.5 seconds to view the message, and this huge photo means your name has to be smaller. The photo appears at the expense of your brand.

Or consider the contractor who uses a picture of a house. It doesn't communicate whether yours is a siding company, a roofing contractor, a window installer, a power washer, a landscaper, or an electrician. After I've spent my 2.5 seconds noticing the house, your brand message is lost amid all of the other things trying to grab my attention.

The best truck wrap design ideas focus on powerful brand integration. National chains have an easier time using photography because, once again, their brand is already known, so their message need not be 100% focused on conveying it. Home service businesses don't have this luxury.

If you feel your wrap needs a photo to help tell your story, then your brand is probably deficient in some way. You shouldn't need a photo of a condenser unit to speak to the idea of air conditioning. Your brand should be able to do that on its own.

## Rule #3: Limit your advertising copy.

There are only three or four things a good wrap needs: strong brand implementation, a tagline, a web address, and maybe a phone number. Bulleted lists have no place on a vehicle. This isn't the Yellow Pages. Would you rather list 10 things no one remembers or convey one or two memorable takeaways? Think of it this way: If this truck were a billboard, how much copy would be on it?

Billboards and vehicle advertising face similar challenges, so they should employ similar strategies. If you prioritize your copy, it will be more effective.

**In general, the hierarchy should be:**

1. **Brand**

2. **Website URL**

3. **Tagline**

4. **Phone number**

That's it. Don't get caught up in putting meaningless phrases and worthless logos on your truck wrap, such as:

- **"100% Guaranteed."** I would hope your work is guaranteed. The problem with this phrase is that it's so overused, it has no real meaning or value.

- **"24-hour service."** This isn't the proper place to advertise this. The homeowner driving next to you likely does not have an emergency at that very second in the middle of the night.

- **"Residential/commercial."** Okay, so you're saying you serve everyone. Why wouldn't I already think that?

- **"No job too small."** A great way to attract the wrong customer.

- **"Scheduled appointments."** Well, I would hope they're scheduled. I don't want you randomly showing up at my door, right?

- **"Sales • Service • Installation."** Wow, so you sell air conditioning equipment, you fix air conditioning equipment, and you install air conditioning equipment? That's amazing! And equally pointless. Of course you do all those things. If you need to list that, something else is wrong.

- **"Financing available."** You haven't sold anyone anything yet, and they don't even know they need financing. Every legitimate company offers financing. This is not unique.

- **Credit card logos.** OMG! You guys take credit cards like every single other reputable contractor? I can't believe that!

- **Angi, Facebook, Instagram, and BBB logos.** Gee, so I can find you on social media platforms and review websites? Nowadays, it should be painfully obvious that a company would be on social media channels.

- **QR codes.** To date, we have never used a QR code on a truck wrap. I find the idea of a driver trying to aim his phone at a moving vehicle to be unrealistic and potentially dangerous. You could make the argument that when stopped in traffic, a potential customer behind you might have the time to scan the QR code. But again, this assumes that the person behind you needs your services right that second. If you accept the premise that truck wraps are brand-building exercises and not an immediate call to action, then I still believe that as long as the URL and/or phone number are there, they'll know how to get in touch with you. Or they'll simply ask their digital assistant to call you.

## Rule #4: Design to stand out, not fit in.

Contrary to popular belief, van graphic design ideas that incorporate diamond plate, carbon fiber, or tribal flames are not effective. The use of flames and ice on your truck wrap does nothing to increase your branding. Instead, it comes at the expense of your branding.

*A clean layout, an iconic mark, and a unique and disruptive color scheme make this a truly memorable brand.*

The big issues you see with these approaches are that everything is fighting for your attention and there is no sense of foreground and background to keep the priorities of the wrap in focus.

By eliminating fills, noisy backgrounds, photos, bevels, and glows, you'll be on your way to designing a wrap that stands out. The truck wrap market is littered with visual noise on so many trucks. The ones with impact are the wraps we can read and remember; they can't help but stand out among the visual clutter. When your wrap makes an impact and deploys your brand in an innovative but simple way, it can't help but stand out because it's unlike what everyone else is doing.

## Rule #5: Simple, legible, and obvious are good.

If the viewer needs to work too hard to figure out the primary brand messaging, it's an opportunity lost. Vehicle advertising isn't like print collateral, where the viewer can stop, absorb the advertising, and try to understand the message. Choose one primary takeaway to communicate to the viewer. Is it obvious, or is it lost in the imagery? Distance legibility is, of course, a primary concern. You have very

*Even though there are several elements comprising this wrap, the background does not compete with the name, allowing it to come forward for great distance legibility while still being disruptive and memorable.*

limited time for the viewer to notice, understand, and remember your brand and message.

Typically, we like to highlight an aspect of your branding in a large, dominant fashion on your truck so that it's easy to read and has maximum impact. That may be the symbol in your logo or your mascot. The repetition of those visual elements is what we hope will become sticky in the homeowner's mind.

Remember how important distance legibility is in your wrap design. This is critical to the success of your outdoor campaign. This probably sounds painfully obvious, but if you can't read your name and what you do, what's the point? Remember that reviewing a proof on your computer or your phone is very different from how it will function outdoors. Step away from your computer screen about 10 feet and see if you can still read your branding clearly. Or try viewing it as a photo on your phone from 10 feet away. If you can't read it there, you'll never read it at a distance outdoors.

Make sure artwork, such as a mascot, is designed for use outdoors. Most mascots based on clip art were not designed to be effective for this specific application, and many of them have legibility and clarity challenges because they were never meant to be used outdoors. Since this art is being viewed from a distance and not on a business card or a website, it needs to be designed with heavier stroke widths that comprise the shape and outline of the mascot. And the details have to be less busy.

One simple way to check the effectiveness of your current truck wrap is to take a photo of it and then convert it to black and white to see if it's still legible. Often, when designs are too dependent on colors, outlines, and other special effects, the design becomes almost illegible in low-light situations. This is an indication of poor contrast in your lettering and is typical of designers with a lack of understanding of how to design effectively for the outdoor medium.

# CHAPTER 8

# COLORS AND YOUR BRAND

# Owning your brand colors.

We've already talked about how to leverage colors to build a more disruptive brand. The biggest takeaway is to be bold, be unique, and develop a set of brand colors that no one in your space has.

That should be painfully obvious as an objective. Fortunately for you, it's really not. In any given market you'll find dozens of companies all using the same color scheme. The obvious colors are red, white, and blue for many home service companies, especially in HVAC.

In this example, there's more than just commonality among the competitors as a fundamental flaw in their color strategy; that particular color scheme is associated with something else other than their businesses: Americana. As such, people look at those colors and subconsciously associate their brands with something else. They've basically helped the viewer to disassociate their brands from who they are.

We recently designed a home service brand for a pest control company. We had presented several unique color schemes based on their market and what we thought could be unique and ownable there. We had pitched blue and orange. The client had retained a marketing coach who suggested red and black instead because "those are the colors that Orkin uses." Why would we ever want your brand to be associated with someone else's brand—who is also an actual competitor? That makes no sense at all.

If someone looks at your brand colors and immediately thinks of something else, then we'd want to change that. The idea is to build brand colors that people associate uniquely with yours.

Think of FedEx and UPS. Your mind has been trained, through repetition, to associate those colors with those brands. As you pick your brand colors, think of how you can build a color palette that doesn't remind people of someone else's brand.

## Color theory and consumers.

Every time a consumer interacts with your brand, they form an impression. Colors will aid in building what that impression means to them and ultimately help convince them to make a purchase. The idea is to create palettes that help in the overall feeling that a consumer gets when interacting with your brand—while simultaneously sparking an element of memorability.

Years ago, we rebranded for an orthopedic surgeon, whose original brand color scheme was red and black. When it comes to health care, red is associated with blood, and black is associated with death. In my mind, the message was "We're going to cut you open, and then you may die." Not exactly the warm, caring notion I'd like to get from my surgeon. So we rebranded him in a blue palette.

All colors are going to have emotions tied to them—some based on a person's unique personality, some more broadly accepted. Red is

*This apple green and dark blue color scheme really stands out in a market littered with red and blue service vans.*

the color of fire and blood. Purple is the color of royalty and luxury. Yellow is a more energetic color. Green generally symbolizes nature, good health, and the environment.

Through repetition, people will remember brand colors before the actual elements of a logo. In fact, research has indicated that color alone can dictate whether a consumer is attracted to a particular brand. When we consider the role of the vehicles and your fleet branding, it's clearly important to consider what we want the takeaway to be for the consumer—while simultaneously associating those colors with you only.

# Through repetition, people will remember brand colors before the actual elements of a logo.

That's not easy to do, but the best advice is to avoid common color palettes. We are constantly trying to find color palettes that seem like they shouldn't even work together but do. A lot of our brands use triads of colors, which allows us to expand the number of possible brand colors that we can build to be uniquely associated with that brand.

## Colors in your marketplace.

Some markets will immediately dictate colors that are off the table for you to use. For example, if you're on the East Coast near Philadelphia, we're not going to recommend that you use orange as one of your primary brand colors because there's already a very large home service company there with orange vans. If we put a brand out there that also uses orange, it will be very difficult for your vans to be distinct enough to not be associated with theirs.

We start the branding process by looking at all the competitors in a market and what colors they are using, and we build our strategy from that vantage point. Usually, we'll see many red and blue color

*We chose the colors for AirCo after reviewing the brand colors of competitors in their market and deciding on a unique set of colors to deploy that would be disruptive and ownable.*

schemes, which we immediately avoid. Many companies are still not wrapping their vehicles and instead use white vans. Those white vans may have brand colors for their lettering, but they are missing the opportunity to stand out. Don't count them out, though. At some point they may get with the times and wrap all their vehicles in their brand colors. So we always consider that.

Once you've eliminated the colors not to use, you can start to think about the colors you can use.

## Colors in other applications.

Certainly, your vehicles remain the most important consideration when choosing your brand colors. But keep in mind how those colors also need to perform in all other applications we talk about in our brand wheel. How will they work on your uniforms? Your website? Your business cards? All those touchpoints matter as well.

As color relates to uniforms, there are more opportunities to be creative with how you outfit your team. As designers, full dye-sublimation shirts allow us to design uniforms that are unique and creative and offer us unlimited color options. If those options are

# Branded, not blanded, uniforms.

Uniforms present a great opportunity to reinforce your brand colors and help make all the employees feel part of the team. The cost of full-color dye-sub shirts has become much more affordable, making them a nice alternative to traditional uniform options.

too flashy for you, then think about the availability of stock-colored shirts, and make sure you can find options to match or complement your brand color scheme.

Branded site signs are also a great way that color can be used in a unique and disruptive manner. Most of the site signs you see have simple white backgrounds and boring logos that blend in. When

*This billboard displays a unique and ownable color palette with simple, easy-to-read brand messaging.*

you use a unique color palette, the viewer is more likely to notice something out of the ordinary and take a second look. The same concept applies to billboards.

You want to make sure your brand colors are heavily integrated into your physical space. Branded signage, wall wraps, carpeting, and paint colors should all be coordinated to reflect your brand. Use your space as an opportunity to reinforce what makes your company unique.

Remember that the goal of brand color choices is to make your brand more unique and disruptive than anyone in your space and to simultaneously deliver brand promise. Your vehicles will be the single most important application of your brand, so colors should be viewed from the vantage point of how well they will work on your truck—and whether they'll be unique enough that people will only associate those brand colors with your brand over time. It's not enough to be just the purple cow. You need to look like a professional home service company.

# Pretty in pink.

"Our previous name (FlowPro Plumbing and Drains) was a tongue twister and a lot of people had difficulty with it. We also wanted a name that aligned with the type of service we provide. The last thing that comes to mind when you think of plumbing is it being 'pristine.' We wanted to set ourselves apart in the industry by going above and beyond to prove that plumbers can, and should, provide a 'white-glove' level of service. We also wanted our color scheme to stand out in our community and appeal to women, hence the pink, since studies have shown that they are the primary decision maker at home.

"We were really surprised by the number of calls we were getting from random people just wanting to tell us how awesome our truck wrap design was! We were also surprised by how our whole team embraced the change and were all in with buying pink accessories. Personalized extension cords, truck bins, phone/tablet chargers— one tech even went with pink hair and has kept it ever since! I think we're in a time where it's finally cool to be different and stand out, and they were all for it!

"Revenue before branding was $650,000 annually. It's been three years since rebranding and we're on pace for $3 million this year. We earned $2.1 million in 2021." —*Angel Blevins, Owner, Pristine Plumbing, Indianapolis, IN*

CHAPTER 9

# MASCOTS IN HOME SERVICE BRANDING

# The origins of mascot-based consumer advertising.

The use of mascots in consumer advertising is certainly not a new idea, with some of the earliest mascots dating back to 1877. One of the first mascots was used by Quaker Oats, when the owner, Henry Seymour, thought a good name for his company would be "Quaker," which in his mind sounded like a company that had nice, honest people and created simple and pure oatmeal. So, the image he created was originally meant to be a visual representation of those ideals.

This was one of the first instances of using a mascot to represent something a company wanted a consumer to feel and to relate it back to a product. Seymour was truly a pioneer in consumer packaging, and he is widely considered to be the "father of mascots."

Elsie the Cow, for Borden Dairy, is another famous mascot. Conceived in the 1930s, she was created to help counter the negative press regarding dairy cows and tuberculosis. An ad agency decided that a friendly cow would help gain the trust of consumers and be a symbol of something wholesome and safe. After its launch, sales skyrocketed, and a survey done in the 1940s showed that 98% of the American public recognized the brand. Imagine how much easier your marketing would be if 98% of the community you served recognized your brand!

The original word "mascot" has its origins in the French word "Mascotte," which means a lucky charm. Mascots certainly can be a lucky charm for home service companies because they help consumers connect with your company and make them feel something about the service you provide. As so many consumer product companies have found, mascots ultimately help sell their product. Whether it is Tony the Tiger or the Michelin Man, some of the most astute brands in the world have embraced mascot branding to help sell more of their products.

It's no different for home service companies. As we talked about earlier, a mascot is another marketing tool to help draw attention to your company and package it in a way that a homeowner might remember and connect with your services and brand promise. It certainly helps provide a more personal feeling for the company and runs opposite of the colder "world-class" corporate approach.

## How does a consumer choose one contractor over another?

With a seemingly endless number of options, homeowners often rely on referrals from their friends or check out online reviews. When they have no references from people they can trust, they rely on a contractor's branding to help make their decision. Think about it: If internet searches, mailbox fliers, and newspaper ads present multiple options for the same services at similar price points, how else do consumers decide which company to call? And if they all looked the same, how would any of them stand out?

Consumers want evidence that a company is professional, trustworthy, and reliable. To stand out, contractors need to do something innovative and different, and not just in terms of company mission and scope. A contractor's branding needs to deliver a powerful message, or consumers won't even bother to pick up the phone.

Branding with a thoughtfully designed mascot can evoke those feelings that homeowners want to associate with a contractor: friendly, honest, approachable, and reliable. A mascot colorfully depicts a company's personality and brand promise, ensuring that it stands out among its competitors and is a company that homeowners can feel comfortable welcoming into their homes. Successful mascot designs are intended to give an "at your service" type of feel. Remember how we talked about consumer bias in chapter 5? This is one way to help counter the consumer bias inherent in purchasing decisions.

## Brands with mascots stand out.

In a crowded market, especially when competitors have dull, poor branding, a mascot resonates well with consumers because it's distinctive. It's impactful in small doses because it's eye-catching and sticks in people's minds. Individuals think that they've seen a mascot "everywhere" or multiple times when, in reality, their only exposure to it was on one truck that rolled through their neighborhood or in one ad that was featured in their local magazine.

There are plenty of clients who have us design their brand and truck wrap using a character or mascot for their one-and-only service truck, but they tell us that customers say, "We see your trucks all the time." They chuckle to themselves since they really only have one vehicle. That's the power of a memorable brand. It sticks out in the minds of consumers and is an uncommon approach to small business marketing. This packs a powerful punch against larger companies with bigger budgets that can afford to put their brand everywhere.

## Mascots break down barriers.

A mascot also enables a new company to break into the market and compete against experienced companies whose names consumers know. This branding style portrays longevity and gives weight to a new name. Nostalgic branding is especially effective because it helps evoke a time when people had a more favorable view of old-school craftsmanship and values.

Mascots' personalities feel relatable, so they resonate with consumers who might be against big businesses or franchises and want to support small local businesses instead. Because their charisma conjures trust, mascots break down barriers between consumers and a company with which they've had no experience. A company with a carefully crafted mascot no longer appears cold, corporate, or crooked.

Of course, a mascot gone wrong won't yield positive reactions like these. If it's too cheesy or amateurish, instead of enhancing a company's professional perception, a mascot can have the opposite effect.

Ultimately, incorporating a mascot into a contractor's branding—when done properly—can yield tremendous success. It can help transform the company's identity by defining the brand promise and building a personality.

## "Mascots don't work."

In 2012, we created one of our first mascot-based HVAC brands for Timo's Air Conditioning & Heating in Palm Springs. At the time, few companies in the country deployed mascots, let alone a nostalgic-based mascot. Since that time, I'd say we've created an additional 750 or so mascot-based brands for home service. So, yes, we do have quite a bit of experience in not only creating mascot brands but in assessing the results over the last decade.

Do they work? That's the big question, right? I hear chatter online and even within some coaching organizations that promote the idea that mascots are not a good idea in the home space.

In the case of Timo's mascot, it sure seems to be working, as it has become the most stolen mascot we've ever created, with over 25 instances of trademark infringement occurring over the years. Expensive lessons were learned by thieves.

I'm not sure about the origins of negativity against mascots. I will say the vast majority of mascots deployed today are not well executed, so that may be part of the reason. Many are poorly drawn or use the same stock clip art that everyone else is using. In those scenarios, yes, poorly executed mascot branding doesn't work. Clip art mascots don't work. Mascots that were never designed for truck wraps don't work. I agree with all those points.

But the fact remains that a well-executed home service brand that utilizes a mascot is proven time and again to work. All you need to do is go back and look at the mascots used in consumer product packaging. Do you believe those companies would spend millions on branding and packaging with mascots if they didn't work?

The key to branded mascots is to be unique with how they are rendered and designed. Make their characteristics memorable and

# Medcalf mascots help sales explode.

"I was blown away at the speed of brand recognition. Most people know who we are and what we do in seconds. We have recently started tracking sales brought in directly from our branding. Also, I feel that the energy of the brand has a positive effect on current and future employees as well as customers. I was on track for around $125,000 gross when we first started the process with KickCharge™. We started in February 2020. We finished the rebrand in February 2021, and we finished 2021 at $1.3 million. Currently, for 2022, we are tracking $4.9 million." —*Brandon Medcalf, Medcalf Heating & Cooling, Terre Haute, IN*

not generic like basic clip art. This is one reason why period-based mascots tend to work so well. In addition to being unique, they evoke feelings of nostalgia and help communicate the notion of better service to the homeowner.

The Goettl mascot helped propel them from $10 million to $200 million in 10 years. Seems to be working well there, I guess, right?

## Scary mascots are counterproductive to brand promise.

As mentioned in chapter 5, beware of aggressive mascots that appear to be ready and able to do bodily harm to the homeowner.

# Don't be generic with your mascot!

I remember working with this client on their mascot-based brand, and they thought the nose was too big. They thought that it was sticking out too much and it should be smaller. The key phrase here is "sticking out." Well, yes, I absolutely want it to be sticking out, and the fact that their attention was drawn to it proves that it was working exactly as I wanted it to. It was memorable! Of course, after rebranding, their sales exploded, and the company is crushing it.

The steroid-fueled musclehead mascot wielding a wrench that doubles as a lethal weapon probably isn't making Mrs. Jones feel super comfortable about who is coming to her home to service her system. Funny, happy penguins are much better choices. They're probably not going to commit assault and battery.

## Mascot styles.

There are different styles and genres of mascots that can be deployed with your branding. Which one is right for you depends on what type of image and vibe you'd like your brand to have. Beyond that, you have to consider which style of mascot might help to convey a brand story you're hoping to leverage from that foundational brand element.

The mascots we've created run the gamut. People often ask me which style works best or has earned the biggest ROI. Honestly, that's hard to say. Regardless of style, as we've discussed in detail, consistency in integration is always a crucial component to the success of a mascot brand. And of course, creating something unique and memorable is very important. It's another reason why generic clip-art-based mascots don't work nearly as well and should be avoided. Here are a few types of mascots:

- **Period-based cartoons.** These mascots are typically used with nostalgia-based brand approaches. They usually deploy aspects that were common from a particular time period, generally the 1940s to late 1950s. Although you could argue that these types of mascots might work better with an older demographic, we've seen no evidence to suggest that their appeal doesn't work across multiple generations. Here's a few types of mascots styles.

- **Modern mascots.** These mascots are more contemporary and don't necessarily deploy styles that are more closely related to nostalgia or a specific time.

- **Illustrative or realistic mascots.** One of the first uses of an illustration-based mascot that we deployed was for Goettl back in 2013. Their particular style was based on how Norman Rockwell might have painted the image of the boy featured in the logo. (That boy was based on the owner's son.)

Of course, you can also have brands based on the likeness of someone, whereby you leverage their notoriety or standing within a community, essentially making them the face of the brand. Such was the case with the branding we executed for Tommy Mello's company, A1 Garage. After a decade of it being featured in their ads and previous truck wraps, we wanted to leverage his likeness and create a warmer, more inviting color palette that still featured him in the branding. Certainly, reproduction challenges can occur in different mediums, so that is something of which to be cognizant. In many instances, however, the brand can function independent of the illustrative mascot and be used without it, depending on the application.

- **Caricature-based mascots.** As we did for A1 Garage, we've created quite a few caricature-based mascots, which are

*This animal-based mascot brand exudes warmth and friendliness. The unique color scheme stands out in a crowded market filled with red, white, and blue.*

based on the likeness of a real person. They're quite memorable, as opposed to common clip-art-based mascots. The elements that comprise the rendering, which is exaggerated, make the mascot and the brand more memorable than something generic or not necessarily based on anyone specific.

• **Animal-based mascots.** Although they're less commonly utilized in home service branding in comparison to mascots based on humans, animal-based mascots are creative, fun, and perhaps even more memorable than human-based mascots. This may be because they are a bit rare. Obviously, this approach is going to pair well with brands that evoke a specific animal in their name. You can also use them to help communicate aspects of a brand promise you are trying to evoke. For example, speed as a brand promise can be communicated with fast animals like horses, roadrunners, birds, and cheetahs. The notion of speed plays well because homeowners are looking for a fast way to get their problems solved and make their pain go away.

*Here's a great example of an inanimate object being used as a mascot to complement the name and the tagline "Comfort Is Only a Heartbeat Away." This company was previously named DS Heating and Air.*

If you're a roofer, animals like turtles and rhinos can help communicate the idea of protection. Owls can evoke wisdom and intelligence. We've also used lots of dog mascots in branding, which personify loyalty and friendliness.

These are all positive characteristics that are attractive to homeowners. Coupling these images with a memorable, unique brand name is something we've always seen perform exceptionally well.

Animals that are also prevalent in the specific geographic region can help create a connection to the community, signaling that the home service company is local and familiar.

• **Inanimate objects.** One fun and unique way to make mascots is to create them out of inanimate objects. They're not modeled after a human technician, so you have more latitude creatively to build something that's going to be very different in any given market in terms of approach. Wrenches, limes, suns—we've done them all, and they always do well for our clients.

## Brand mascots made into real, physical mascots.

Having your brand mascot made into a physical mascot is a great way to reinforce your branding and draw crowds to your public events. Who doesn't love having their kids take pictures with a cute, fun mascot? We've had many clients get their mascots made into physical mascots and then use them at home shows and community events. They become magnets that draw people to their booths. People are always happy to have their pictures taken with them. These types of events are great brand-building exercises to help the community connect with your company while leaving them with a memorable impression and experience.

The cost for developing your mascot into a physical mascot ranges depending on the complexity, but most of the ones our clients have done are in the range of $5,000 to $7,500.

We've also had many clients get their mascot made into stuffed animals and give them out at home shows or at the end of every service call.

## Bottom line: It works.

There is some chatter in various Facebook groups for home service company owners about mascots being played out. Certainly, the use of mascots has become more prevalent. Perhaps we've had something to do with that perception, since we've created many home service mascots, and many in the home service industry follow our work. But the reality is that in most markets, mascots can still be very effective, especially when executed correctly. So many are not, which leaves an opportunity for you to have a brand that features a mascot that is professionally done. But if there are already many similarly styled mascots in your space, then you will need to think differently about how you execute a mascot. Whether it is a big-headed Buehler dude or a boy holding a flashlight, always keep the idea of disruption top-of-mind when considering your strategy.

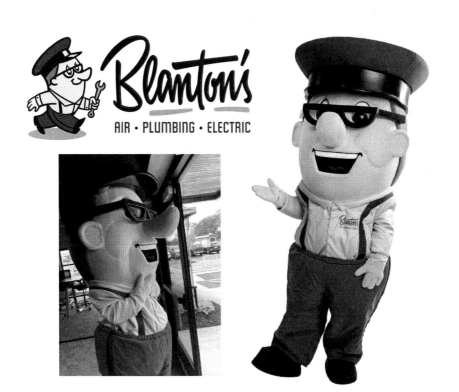

*The "Coolidge" mascot for Blanton's has been a huge hit at various parades and home shows.*

*The friendly bear mascot we created for Apex Plumbing was made into a stuffed animal. These toy bears make great gifts for homeowners with children, creating a regular positive reinforcement of the brand.*

CHAPTER 10

# WHERE TO BUILD YOUR BRAND

# Okay, I'm ready to brand!

As the owner of a home service company, you're probably familiar with some of the various options for where you might go to build your brand. Typical options include your sign or truck wrap company, a graphic designer, a branding agency, or crowdsourced options. Maybe your web design company says they can help. Or the company doing your billboards. Of course, your nephew or niece who is "really good at Photoshop" is also a consideration.

Wow, that's a lot of people who say they can build a brand for your most critical asset, which is, of course, your brand. With prices for their services running the gamut, who would be the best partner for you in this endeavor?

Clearly, experience is a critical factor. I look at a brand as the heart of your marketing efforts. If your business needed surgery on its heart, you'd probably want to find a surgeon with the most experience who had done many other successful heart surgeries. As a double bypass surgery survivor myself, I thoroughly researched my surgeon before choosing him. As a business owner, you should search with the same diligence. Look for a partner who does this frequently and has had great success.

It's also important to make sure you like the work in their portfolio. That is always a good indication of whether or not they're capable. Whenever possible, you want their work to be similar to your vision of your brand.

Speak to owners of companies they've worked for and ask about the process. Of course, experience with home service businesses like yours is important as well.

But the key to a successful brand company is not just understanding your business, how you sell and communicate with your customers, and what your customer looks like. It's understanding how this new brand needs to live and breathe on all the different touchpoints that will integrate this new logo. Remember the brand wheel we talked about in chapter 1? That's important to get right. If they get the foundation wrong, that wheel is never going to spin correctly. A deep understanding of how well this new logo needs to function, from your truck wraps to your website and everything in between, is the difference between an amateur and a professional.

Let's talk about some of the options you have when it comes to building your brand.

## Traditional graphic designers.

When it comes to traditional graphic designers, beware that most are not brand designers. Although related, logo design is a very unique skill set that most graphic designers don't possess. They may be quite skilled at designing websites, brochures, and advertisements, but sometimes they are in over their heads when it comes to branding. Many are great at brand integration—taking a logo and creating the rest of the marketing that supports that brand—but not as good at creating the original logo. This is especially true for logos that require original illustration work, which is a separate skill set. Case in point: We recently hired a brand designer for our agency. Over 200 graphic designers applied, all of whom said they could do logo design. Out of 200, only two were qualified and demonstrated in their portfolio a deep understanding of how to create compelling brands.

## Digital marketing companies.

Most digital marketing companies are not qualified to take on branding tasks for your business. Perhaps they have web designers on staff, but just as a graphic designer is probably not a logo designer, the same holds true for web designers. With the right branding, a good digital agency with a solid creative team can make a great website with your new brand. But I wouldn't expect them to be able to create a compelling brand and brand strategy. Typically, that's not in their wheelhouse. Additionally, most are not experienced in what is needed from a foundational standpoint in creating a brand that will function well on all the other non-digital applications that your business will need. (Like a truck wrap.)

## Sign and wrap companies.

Can your sign and wrap company make a great brand for you? In many instances, no, they can't. Most sign and wrap companies, while being good at printing and installing wraps, aren't the most qualified to offer you branding advice. Of course, there are a few that can blend solid design principles and help build the foundation of an effective brand. But if you were to judge most by the wraps they've designed and the logos they've created, you'll rarely see an effective brand strategy come from a sign company. I've spent over two decades teaching and educating sign companies on brand theory and fundamentals, and the skills—or lack thereof—run the gamut.

This is largely an industry issue. While there are many reasons for this, unlike most trades, there is absolutely no barrier to entry to own and operate a sign company. No design education or marketing degree is needed, and with some informal training, you can begin printing and installing signs and wraps. Many of these companies simply don't have the resources needed to effectively research, plan, and execute a unique and compelling brand strategy for you. They're in the business to print and install things, not labor every detail of how your brand needs to appear in multiple environments and speak to your target audience.

Remember, your logo is more than just a cool wrap design. It's also how well it performs on all your other channels. Typically, wrap companies are not going deep into foreseeing how all those integrations work for your brand, which can make that brand wheel not spin very well.

Not every budget allows you to work with a qualified branding agency. In that case, it's important to study and review the portfolios of any potential sign and wrap companies you are considering and to make sure that they have work in their portfolios that adheres to the fundamentals of effective branding, as detailed in chapters 5 and 6.

## Crowdsourcing your brand.

With the abundance of crowdsourcing sites on the internet, it may seem like a good idea to have a contest for the creation of your brand. The contest winner gets paid, and you get dozens of logo ideas for free. *What could possibly go wrong?*

Oh, lots of things can go wrong. You have no idea about the experience, expertise, or business ethics of any of the participants. You also have no real way of trusting that any of their designs is the right solution for your business.

But the most troubling aspect is that you have no way of knowing if the artwork they present to you as your shiny new brand is original or simply stolen from someone else. That's one of the big challenges with crowdsourcing, and if you think about the math for any one of the "designers" who participate in this endeavor,

*The original crowdsourced logo design and truck wrap generated zero phone calls in one year. The newly redesigned brand and truck wrap generated over 80 phone calls within the first nine months after launch.*

it's clear why this happens. How much time can you expect them to spend on something that they are competing with dozens of other designers for? If theirs is not chosen, they get paid zero. It becomes a question of how many contests they can participate in, in the hopes they'll eventually win one and get paid. So shortcuts must be taken. No research can be done. Why would they invest a significant amount of time on something they have little chance of ever being paid for?

Trademark infringement tends to run rampant on sites like this. How do I know? Because our clients have had their brands, mascots, and truck wraps resold to countless people. Copyright infringement is a serious issue, and unfortunately, a business may learn about its logo infringement only after cease-and-desist letters arrive from another company's attorney. When those letters arrive, think about how expensive it's going to be to redo everything that uses this stolen logo, not to mention the potential damages the trademark owner may demand.

Is the crowdsourcing site going to reimburse you for your expenses to redo everything? Nope, their contracts absolve them of all liability for such events. Is the designer overseas going to reimburse you? I'm pretty sure you're out of luck.

In all likelihood, you will also never speak directly to the designer. If you're truly looking to take your business to a higher level, it's important to discuss your plans verbally and spend a lot of time fleshing out your vision, working through a creative brief, and fully discussing the target demographic your brand should appeal to. Crowdsourcing sites usually don't allow that type of two-way communication.

Have there been people in home service businesses who have gone that route and arrived at something that works for their business? Sure. If you have no budget set aside at the time of your startup, this may be the best option available to you. Not everyone can afford a design agency, and this is a quick way to at least get something.

I do believe the negatives outweigh the benefits, but if it's your only option and you understand the potential pitfalls, it's probably better than having your nephew design your logo. The higher reward you offer for the contest winner, the higher the likelihood of getting a better brand. A $99 logo is typically going to be worth about what you pay for it.

If you accept the premise that your brand is perhaps the single most important foundation of your overall marketing strategy, does it make any sense at all to risk it with perhaps the least qualified source? We have rebranded dozens of companies that went that route, and I can tell you, it winds up costing them so much more in the long run than just doing it right in the first place. We have a lot of data to prove this. I wish we didn't, though. I wish those companies hadn't wasted their money.

## Design and branding agencies.

Of course, I may be a bit biased toward recommending that you consider working with a branding or design agency when building your brand. Branding agencies are going to have a lot of experience creating and implementing brands, as well as an in-depth understanding of brand integration across multiple channels. They are typically staffed with a solid creative team who can assist in building and naming your brand. That team will consist of illustrators who can create original art for your brand—and not rely on clip art like many of the alternative providers we just discussed.

When it comes to developing a more comprehensive brand story that can be told not only with effective visuals but in the words and voice of your brand, a design agency is going to be the best partner to build a professional brand.

The downside of design agencies is that they're likely going to be your most expensive option, and not all are specifically suited to the home service market. One of the most important integrations of your brand is your truck wrap, so experience in that medium is an important consideration. Surprisingly, many agencies don't have much real-world experience in branding integration on vehicles.

**Questions to ask before signing a contract for branding services:**

- **Will the price be a fixed dollar amount or an hourly rate?** This question is important, as it helps determine your anticipated costs. We charge a fee that includes a predetermined number of hours that we expect to need to complete the work. The hours we budget include time for revisions and additional options if needed. It is extremely rare for us to go over budget, and if your design partner is skilled and does the proper homework before commencing, they shouldn't go over budget.

- **Who will own the rights to the completed artwork?** This may seem obvious, but make sure your ownership rights to your new logo are clearly defined.

- **Who will own the rights to the rejected artwork?** If the designers are presenting multiple options that are not chosen, find out who maintains ownership of the unused sketches.

- **What files will be supplied to you when the job is complete?**

- **Who will produce the work? Will it be outsourced?** This question is important because it helps provide accountability on the work being produced and indicates who would ultimately be responsible were the art to infringe on the rights of someone else.

- **Will the artwork be original or based on clip art?** If it is based on clip art, be aware that you will not be able to trademark your logo. Clip art is considered public domain, and websites that sell clip art specifically state in their terms that the art should not be used for logos and that they own the rights to that clip art. Some very large home service companies use generic clip art for their logo. That means that a new company could start in the same market using the same clip art, and there is not a thing that could be done to prevent that company from using it.

- **How many concepts will be presented to you?** This will help give you a sense of how many ideas you'll see. Bear in mind that more concepts are not necessarily an indication of value. If you get 10 options and nine are awful, that's not as useful as two or three solid concepts. Typically, the crowdsource route will result in dozens of options, with scant few viable ones.

- **How will the concepts be presented?** If you own a home service business, seeing the concepts on an actual truck is so important since it's the single most critical application of your brand. I would recommend you hire a company that presents each option on an actual truck so you can better understand how it might be integrated into your fleet.

- **How many revisions will you be able to request if you don't like the initial concepts?** Within our budgets, we essentially have unlimited revisions. Once our budgeted time is exceeded, then we would need to charge for them. We budget enough time in the event that the initial concepts don't meet expectations, but if the design team does their job, they really shouldn't require unlimited revisions.

- **What will be your financial obligation, should you decide to kill the project once work has commenced?**

- **Will the agency create a brand guidebook or style guide that illustrates how your brand elements should or should not be implemented across various platforms?**

- **What is the agency's typical fail ratio?** This lets you know how often they were unable to arrive at a branding solution that their clients found satisfactory. It stands to reason that the more brands they create, the less likely they might be to have any failures. When crowdsourcing, this is not a question you'll get an answer to. Our fail ratio is probably around 1 in 100. I'm really proud of the fact that it very rarely happens. But since we've created over 2,000 brands, our success rate is exceptional.

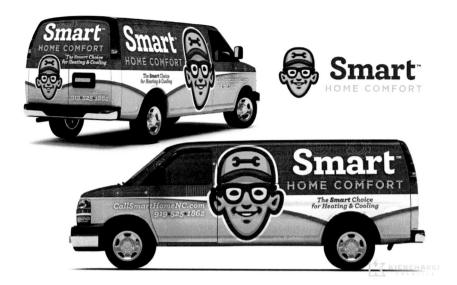

*Disruption takes guts. Not every client is ready to truly disrupt, so be cognizant of what your comfort zone is and how far outside of it you're willing to go. This design was really different in its market, which is exactly why we wanted to go in that direction.*

## Working with your design partner.

Once you choose a design partner, their job is to figure out who your ideal market is, what they like, and how to craft messages that connect with that audience. Their job is not to design a logo that you like. That's an audience of one.

Far too many owners approach branding with the mindset that their brand needs to be driven by what they like, and they fail to consider what Mrs. Jones likes. She is 35-55, is married, has two kids in college, owns a dog, has three cars, and has a household income of $150,000-$250,000 a year.

What does she like? Which colors? What is she afraid of? How do we create empathy with her and make her care about our brand? These are the questions that your design agency should ask you. Of course, your input is important for themes, styles, and genres. But these questions must be framed with the audience in mind.

Over the years, I've had clients who wanted to make their brands all about what they liked. But if what they liked wasn't the same as what Mrs. Jones liked, then it was my job to tell them that. That's what you should expect from your design partner.

Conversely, if you believe you know exactly what you want for your brand, then I'd highly recommend **not hiring a design agency at all** and simply crowdsourcing your logo. There are going to be plenty of people in that space happy to cash your check and give you exactly what you ask for—despite it not being what you need,

## A camel is a horse designed by a committee.

As you go through the process of rebranding, here's a word of caution about sharing concepts with others and soliciting feedback from employees or friends who are not familiar with the strategies and recommendations regarding your branding.

# The more disruptive your brand, the fewer people will truly get what it is you're trying to do.

Visionaries are often mocked for their ideas that run contrary to the norm. But to be disruptive—especially as it relates to branding— **the idea is to stand out, not fit in**. That takes courage because, quite often, the people you ask for opinions are uncomfortable with change, and they're usually quite uncomfortable with something atypical. This is especially true when it comes to employees, who are inherently afraid of any change and much prefer the comfort of the status quo.

The more disruptive your brand, the fewer people will truly get what it is you're trying to do. Why? Well, quite simply, because it's not "normal." Because it feels different from what brands are "supposed" to do. And that's why we're recommending this strategy: because it is different, unexpected, and unnatural. That's the difference between blanding and branding.

I clearly remember when we launched the new branding for Buehler Air brand referenced earlier in this book. Everyone told Buehler that the big head mascot on the side of his van was too big. He even called me frantically the day his first three vans were getting wrapped: "Dan, the head is too big on the van. We need to make it smaller."

Fortunately, I had developed a friendship with Buehler during the rebranding process and was able to share my thoughts without needing to sugarcoat them. So, I very matter-of-factly replied: "Dude, we are not changing the size of the fucking head."

I went a little more in detail about why we weren't going to do such a dumb thing, and he begrudgingly relented. The rest, as they say, is history. After the business doubled in one year, my point was proven. Everyone knows the Buehler brand because of those big heads.

Keep in mind that most people will be unable to see the true vision and brand story from the concepts that you present to them. So, essentially, it falls into the category of judging a book by its cover when no one's been able to even read the story, let alone the first chapter.

# The more people who give input during the process, the less effective the branding becomes.

As an owner, you may want to get other people's buy-ins before making a change. In our experience, as noted earlier, the more people who give input during the process, the less effective the branding becomes. It is extremely rare to get everyone on board with a concept. In fact, some of our most successful brands were never shared with anyone before the brand launch announcement. And some of our most successful brands were universally panned

# Jay's brand and image get a fresh, streamlined new look.

The original truck wrap for this business exhibited classic challenges seen often in many home service truck wraps. The wrap itself was very busy, and the brand name was difficult to read. Additionally, the numerous background elements were competing with the brand. Besides those design issues, there was a problem with the naming that we hoped to solve by spelling out their name as "Jay's" instead of "J's" and giving the visual of a bird to aid in recognition.

Although the owner heard quite often, "We see your trucks everywhere," the design and naming problems needed to be solved in order to maximize the opportunity that a more disruptive truck wrap provides.

A professional design agency should always make sure your investment in marketing is going to yield the maximum returns.

by people who viewed the concepts before the launch. Later, they got it and understood the story behind the brand. Bear in mind as well that your technicians are not the primary audience that the brand is intended for. Remember, it's Mrs. Jones who makes most of the purchasing decisions for her household.

Should you decide to share, please be mindful of such reactions. **When everyone zigs, don't be afraid to zag. That's what propels great companies with visionary leadership. And that's why you are here.**

## Who you ask matters.

I'd also be cautious regarding the qualifications of who you ask for advice, especially as it relates to various coaches and similar organizations in the home service space. Most coaches for home service are amazing when it comes to strategies for operation issues for your business. They have great insights on performance metrics, sales techniques, operations, and staffing. But many are inexperienced with branding fundamentals and how to truly develop unique and disruptive branding strategies.

The best coaches are the ones who understand that they can't be experts on every aspect of running your business and who recommend that you partner with companies that excel in areas outside their wheelhouse. That's not a sign of weakness. On the contrary—it's a sign that they have your best interests in mind.

We've unfortunately seen the results of the poor branding advice that's been given to our clients by various coaching organizations. Sadly, they've been very expensive lessons—not just in the hard cost of redoing all their branding elements, but in the lost revenue and missed opportunities. Truthfully, it makes me angry to see the livelihoods of people's businesses be given so little regard and to realize how much people have paid for this poor advice.

Like I said earlier, the responsibility of a person giving branding advice is huge. They should be thinking that lives are at stake, and if they're going to be making recommendations, they had better know what they're doing. Otherwise, let the pros handle it.

# CHAPTER 11

# LAUNCHING YOUR NEW BRAND

# The fresh start.

No matter how large or small your business is, any brand redesign means a lot of trauma to the business—financial and otherwise. It's not a proposition that should ever be entered into lightly. It's a big endeavor that takes a lot of work to properly implement. Your designer or agency needs to understand the implications of your new brand and develop a plan for integration that includes a strategy for brand rollout.

Most of the time, it is nearly impossible for small businesses to simply erase all uses of their previous brand all at once. Not only are the logistics challenging, but it is not financially prudent to do a clean-slate rollout of your new brand. Your old brand has been implemented in too many ways across too many platforms. Getting rid of it immediately isn't always possible.

Having rebranded thousands of small businesses, I'm aware of how traumatic this change can be. Usually, the old brand shows up on everything—including uniforms, trucks, signs, and the website. What we recommend is to draw a line in the sand and, from this point forward, to make sure that everything utilizes the new brand and integrates it as things are updated. A new website design should contain the new brand. Vehicles, as they are replaced, should be wrapped with the new logo. Certainly, some things are less expensive to change and more important, like changing the company stationery and business cards to reflect the new brand. Other things can be rolled out over time.

## Rolling out your new brand.

Creating a new brand is a major milestone. As a company that went through the rebranding process ourselves, we know how challenging it can be. But you'll find the rewards to be well worth the challenge if you roll out your new brand properly.

From your business cards to your fleet of service vehicles, your company's name and logo live on countless platforms. Due to the ubiquity of your brand, being able to just flip the switch on your new brand and change everything simultaneously is highly unrealistic. Instead, you should roll out your new brand in a reasonable timeframe and manner. Otherwise, you run the risk of confusing your current and potential customers with multiple versions of your brand in the marketplace.

Effectively introducing your new brand to the world requires careful planning and implementation. This is where our team of branding experts has your back. With a prioritized brand implementation checklist and budget, you can implement your new look in a manageable way—while still causing the positive disruption you want to achieve.

Use this chapter as a checklist to guide you through tackling the conversion.

## Brand announcements.

Loyal customers deserve to be the first to know about your new brand so that the different look doesn't cause confusion or raise concern. From a blog post to a letter or email—regardless of how you choose to announce your new brand, you must explain the reason why your company rebranded and what the new brand represents for your team and your customers. Reiterate that, despite its new look, nothing else about your company has changed. Reassure your customers that you're still the company they've come to know and that you will continue to deliver the service they trust.

One other important note in the announcement, especially if there is a name change, is to make sure you address your customer's home service warranties—and that they will still be honored. You can also tell your customers that they may see the new and old brands in the marketplace simultaneously while you update your look.

Here's part of the announcement we wrote for Colepepper Plumbing & Drains' brand launch: "We might have done a 180 with our look, but our valued service hasn't changed a bit. We believe the new brand and website will only enhance the relationships we've built with our customers in San Diego, CA, and across our service area. We are fully committed to leading the industry and adapting our

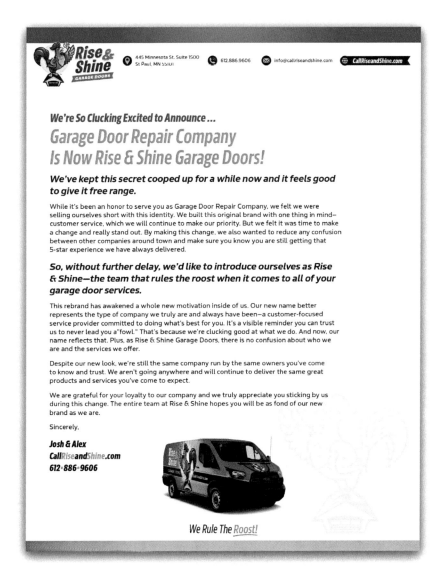

*Here's an example of a brand announcement letter, which we wrote and produced for the launch of Rise & Shine Garage Doors.*

business to best serve our customers, and these changes are a true testament to that."

In addition, spread the word via email (don't forget to update the logo in the email template, if you have one), and I strongly recommend a standard mailing for your existing customers. You can send this mailing (typically a letter in a standard envelope on new letterhead) to not only alert them of the brand change but perhaps include an offer to commemorate the occasion.

A news release is worth considering, particularly if your new identity rollout is announced in conjunction with something that's of public interest, such as celebrating an anniversary, moving into a new office, sponsoring a community event or fundraiser, partnering with another business, expanding services, or adding staff.

## Business cards and stationery.

This is a no-brainer. If handing a business card to a lead is a common first interaction for your employees, the cards must be redesigned with the new brand immediately. Make it count: Get creative with the use of the logo and brand colors, and think differently. Using two-sided cards, rounded corners, unique paper stocks, and spot UV printing are ways to make business cards beautiful.

It's simple and relatively inexpensive to implement new branding on letterhead and business forms. Since this stationery is a regular, frequent part of customer interactions, put this item high on your brand refresh checklist.

## Signage.

Though it's costly, it's important for signage to match the new brand. Resist the urge to modify the logo's proportions to fit the available space. Instead, modify the sign accordingly to accommodate the logo, and use the space as effectively as possible. Remember, it's less important to prominently display a website URL and phone number on signs when the customer is already at your location. Instead, include a sign that's professionally designed in your brand implementation plan and budget.

## Vehicles.

Company vehicles are like moving billboards. Take advantage of this unique yet cost-efficient way to reveal your brand to a large number of people. When designed properly, vehicle wraps are highly effective. Ensure that the design stands out with the logo displayed clearly so that it won't be easily forgotten.

Ideally, when budget allows, you can make the biggest impact by rolling out rebranded vehicles all at once. This can be costly and time-consuming for a company with a large fleet. Tackle updating vehicle wraps by implementing the new brand only on new vehicles or stripping off old lettering and replacing it with the redesigned wrap.

## Uniforms.

Since your employees are your brand ambassadors, putting the new brand on their uniforms is an important step in your brand implementation process. Ensure that they are dressed neatly and professionally. Integrate the brand colors into the design, and avoid adding details like the phone number and website address—just the logo will do.

## Website.

Replace the logo on your company website as soon as the new brand is introduced. Full brand integration should follow soon after, with a website redesign that implements colors, icons, and typography that coordinate with the new logo. The new website should relay your brand promise, making the brand shine. Treat the website like the virtual front door that prospective customers enter the first time they interact with you.

Don't make the mistake of simply swapping your old logo with your new one and calling that a website rebrand. A branded site fully incorporates the new identity visually and in its voice.

## Social media.

Social media networks are an obvious place to announce the change. Ensure that the new logo is plugged into social media graphics when the brand launches. Remember to update your company's presence on all of your existing channels. Now is the perfect opportunity to start an account with your new brand if one doesn't already exist—as long as it is a relevant channel for your company to communicate on.

**Social media channels include but are not limited to:**

- **Facebook**
- **Instagram**
- **Google Business Profile**
- **LinkedIn**
- **YouTube**
- **Twitter**
- **Pinterest**
- **TikTok**

Social media may be where a potential customer decides to search your company name for the first time to get to know who you are. It's important that your brand is portrayed accurately.

## Print collateral.

Print collateral, such as brochures and sell sheets, also need to be updated with your new brand. In addition to the design, take this as an opportunity to review your print collateral's copy and overall messaging. Do they reflect your brand promise and differentiators?

*This is the Facebook cover image we created for On the Double! after we rebranded and renamed the company. In this case, featuring the old logo helped consumers make the connection to the new company.*

If not, it's time to refresh them. Don't forget about updating your maintenance agreement brochures. This will make it easier for the technician to sell the plans to a homeowner. Update all equipment stickers with the new branding as well.

## Brand launch assets.

Introducing your new brand to current and potential customers requires its own planning and communications strategy. The announcement process should begin when the brand makes its public debut—typically when the first wrapped vehicle hits the streets. Use these tactics to ensure there's no confusion. You want the public to know that you're the same trusted team delivering the same level of service your customers expect and appreciate.

Inform employees and existing customers first. Tell them that your brand evolution is an improvement that was only made possible thanks to their loyal patronage. They'll help you spread the word as well. Typical assets include:

- **Email (to existing customers)**
- **Letter or postcard (to existing customers)**
- **Direct mail with special offer (in your service area)**
- **Press releases**
- **Community engagement.** To leverage your brand, sponsor activities in a public space to engage your target audience.
- **Social media promotion**

## Be methodical in your rollout.

Care must be taken when you roll out your new brand. It must be done in an organized, methodical fashion. The good news is that if you do it right, you will not miss a beat in your sales—and it will be a smooth transition.

CHAPTER 12

# TRADEMARKING AND YOUR BRAND

# Protecting your branding investment.

Protecting your business' intellectual property has never been more important than it is today. The downside of the internet is that it has made it much easier for infringement to occur. It's almost like the Wild West nowadays, with tons of unscrupulous "designers"—and even business owners—who don't understand trademarks and who wrongly assume everything they find in a Google image search is fair game.

Well, it's not. This can be a very expensive lesson to learn if you're on the receiving side of that cease-and-desist letter. So how do you stay out of trouble? The best advice I can give is to not crowdsource your branding and to hire a professional. Of course, that's easy for me to say. But of the hundreds of infringements I've seen in my professional career, easily 90% of them originated from either a crowdsourced designer or other sign or wrap companies.

It's awful when my clients need to send out a cease-and-desist letter to another small business that has unwittingly been using my client's intellectual property. It's a waste of resources, time, and most of all money.

It's not just artwork that needs to be looked at when branding, but names as well. We've definitely seen more and more private equity firms flexing on protecting names that they have trademarks on. And let's face it, they usually have an army of lawyers on staff who can make your life miserable pretty quickly.

It's imperative that you understand what's involved with a trademark and how you can protect yourself and your business. I'm not a trademark lawyer, but we do work with one frequently who handles all our logo and trademark tasks on behalf of our clients, as well as (sadly) all the cease-and-desist and infringement claims for them, too. So, I asked **Charles Internicola**, the founder of **Internicola Law**, a national franchise and trademark law firm (franchiselawsolutions. com), to write an extensive Q&A to explain everything you need to know. Charles and his team are amazing professionals.

## What is a trademark?

A trademark can be the name of your business and/or a logo that you use to identify it. More specifically, a trademark is a word, a logo, or a combined word and logo that identifies your business to the public and your customers. Most commonly, your trademark will be the name of your business and the logo that you use to represent and identify it. A trademark may also include slogans that you use in the identification of your business.

As a business owner, protecting your trademark is a critical task. The best way to do this is through registration with the United States Patent and Trademark Office (USPTO). Not every USPTO trademark registration is as valuable as others. How you apply for trademark registration and the classifications that you use are as important as obtaining registration itself.

## What are the different types of trademarks?

A trademark may be a word mark, such as the name of your business; a logo mark such as the image that you use to represent your business; or a combined word and logo mark, which is the name of your business combined with your logo. Word marks are not limited to the name of your business and may include unique terms that you use in association with your business. Colors may also be trademarked as part of your overall logo and, in certain instances, as a part of your business. A good example of a color that is trademarked is the shade of blue used by Tiffany & Co. on its boxes.

# How is a trademark protected?

Trademark protection comes in two different forms: passively through your use of a trademark or actively through USPTO trademark registration.

## 1. COMMON-LAW TRADEMARK PROTECTION

When you use your trademark in commerce (i.e., to represent your business), you may automatically acquire common-law trademark rights. Under the law, if you are the first business to use your trademark within a particular geographic area, then by operation of law, your rights to the trademark will be viewed as superior to those of a competitor who comes along later.

The advantage of common-law trademark protection is that it happens automatically. The disadvantage is that it is extremely limited in both geography (the specific area where you conduct your business) and legal protections (the types of legal actions that you may take in stopping competitors from using your trademark).

## 2. USPTO REGISTRATION PROTECTION

Registration of your trademark with the USPTO will afford your trademark the strongest form of protection. USPTO registration means that a formal trademark registration application has been filed with the USPTO and that an examining attorney at the USPTO has reviewed and granted your trademark registration. The advantage of USPTO registration is that your trademark will be afforded nationwide protection: No matter where you're located or where you operate, your competitors will be prohibited from adopting or copying your trademark. From a legal protection standpoint, there is no disadvantage to USPTO trademark registration.

Whether your business operates locally, is national, or is a franchise system, USPTO trademark registration is necessary to protect your brand. Relying on common-law trademark protection alone is not a viable option.

## TM vs. ®: What symbol should I use with my trademark to let everyone know it's protected?

If your trademark has not yet been registered with the USPTO, you should use the TM symbol. By using the TM symbol, you are signifying to others that you are claiming common-law rights to your trademark. Once your trademark is registered with the USPTO, you should be using the ® symbol.

Using the TM and ® symbols is an important part of protecting your trademark, informing the public of your legal rights, and creating legal consequences if anyone disregards your rights.

## What are the steps to obtaining USPTO trademark registration?

### 1. TRADEMARK REVIEW

Initially, your attorney will review the trademarks that you currently use. These trademarks are typically composed of the name of your business (your word mark) and your logo. Information that your attorney will ask for during the initial review of your trademarks might include:

**YOUR FIRST USE:** the date that you first used your trademark in commerce. This is typically the date when you started your business (assuming that you are using the same name now) and when you first used your logo. Your date of first use is important and has legal consequences.

**YOUR PRODUCTS AND SERVICES:** the products that your business sells or produces and/or the services that your business provides. This is important because when you apply for USPTO trademark registration, your application and your trademark protection will be specific to your industry and the types of products and/or services that your business provides. For example, if your company provides HVAC and plumbing services, even though your word mark may be granted USPTO protection, it is entirely possible that a business in a completely different industry (e.g., a restaurant) may be granted USPTO registration for an identical word mark.

**SAMPLES:** As part of your USPTO trademark application, your attorney will need to submit samples showing how you use your trademarks in commerce (such as images of your branded vehicles, uniforms, and website).

## 2. PRELIMINARY SEARCH

The biggest obstacle to obtaining USPTO registration is the existence of a competing trademark or logo that has already been registered with the USPTO. If a competing business or a business in an industry similar to yours has already obtained or filed for USPTO registration, chances are that your registration application will be rejected. Prior to filing your trademark registration, your lawyer will conduct a preliminary trademark search commonly called a knockout search. If an identical or highly similar word mark shows up in the knockout search, your lawyer should let you know. Because a knockout search is a basic search, it is possible that competing marks may not show up. So, while a knockout search is preliminary and not 100%, it's nevertheless a cost-effective step. Your attorney can order more detailed, third-party generated searches, but these searches are expensive and usually not cost-effective.

## 3. USPTO TRADEMARK APPLICATION PREPARATION

Once the knockout search is complete, your attorney will prepare your USPTO registration application, which will be filed online. Important information about your application includes:

**FILING FEES:** Separate from the legal fee that you will pay to your attorney, you will also be required to pay a filing fee to the USPTO. The USPTO filing fee is $225 per trademark application, per class. Consider that, in most instances, you will be filing two trademark applications: one for your word mark (without the logo) and one for your combined word and logo mark. Since logos change over time, it's important to obtain registration of your word mark by itself. If your business operates in more than one industry (e.g., not only do you own a restaurant but you also sell prepackaged food distributed through stores) then you will be required to file for two classifications, which means the USPTO filing fee would be $550 ($225 x 2 classes) for each trademark.

## 4. APPOINTMENT OF AN EXAMINING ATTORNEY

Once your USPTO trademark application is filed, the next step relates to the USPTO's appointment of an examining attorney, which takes about four months. Once appointed, the examining attorney will review your trademark application and make a determination as to whether or not they will approve your trademarks for registration. The examining attorney has two primary responsibilities:

- Determining whether or not your trademark meets the legal criteria for registration. Trademarks that are descriptive (i.e., your business name is just a description of your business, such as Healthy Food Restaurant for a restaurant or Prompt Plumbing for a plumbing service) are not afforded legal trademark protection.

- Determining whether or not there are any conflicting trademarks that are already registered or on file with the USPTO. At this stage, the examining attorney will search the USPTO database to determine if your trademark is confusingly similar to trademarks that have already been registered.

## 5. RESPONSE TO OFFICE ACTION LETTER

If the examining attorney does not approve your application, you will receive an office action letter. Once this letter is issued, your attorney will have six months to respond. Your attorney's response will depend on the reason for the examining attorney's disapproval. For example, if there are conflicting marks, your attorney may cite legal arguments as to why the marks are not confusingly similar.

## 6. PUBLICATION

After the examining attorney approves your trademark application for registration (typically after your attorney overcomes any objections and issues raised by the examining attorney in the office action letter), the examining attorney will schedule your trademark application to be published in the *Trademark Official Gazette*. This publication notifies the public that unless someone has an objection, your trademark will be granted registration. The *Gazette* is monitored, and if a company believes that your registration may be confusingly similar to their mark (even though the examining attorney did not), they may file a formal objection to your trademark registration. There are other reasons why someone may object to your trademark registration, such as if they believe your trademark is defamatory.

## How long does it take to register a trademark?

USPTO trademark registration typically occurs within 12 months of your initial application. However, variables that affect this timing include whether or not the examining attorney has issued an office action letter, the nature of the letter, and the timing of your attorney's response to the letter.

## How long does USPTO trademark protection last?

USPTO trademark registration can last for an indefinite period. However, to maintain your USPTO trademark registration, you will be required to make periodic filings with the USPTO, and you must protect and enforce your trademark rights against other businesses.

Maintenance filings that must be filed with the USPTO to maintain your trademark registration include:

- **DECLARATION OF CONTINUED USE (SECTION 8 DECLARATION):** A declaration of continued use must be filed with the USPTO before the end of the sixth year following the registration of your trademark.

- **COMBINED DECLARATION OF CONTINUED USE AND RENEWAL (SECTION 8 AND SECTION 9 DECLARATIONS):** A combined Section 8 and Section 9 declaration of continued use of your trademark and application for renewal must be filed before the end of every 10-year period following the trademark registration date.

## What happens if another business is using my trademark?

If another business has copied your trademark or is using a word mark or logo that is confusingly similar to yours, you may have a claim for trademark infringement. If you have obtained USPTO trademark registration, you will have stronger rights than if you just have a common-law trademark. The next step would be to send a cease-and-desist notice, in which you inform the other business of your claim and demand that they stop using the similar trademarks. Since there are many variables involved, it's important to first speak with a trademark lawyer. Factors that will be relevant in whether or not you should send a cease-and-desist notice include:

- **Whether or not your trademark is registered with the USPTO**

- **Where the competing business is located (Is it operating in your market or another part of the country?)**

- **Whether or not the competing business obtained USPTO registration**

- **When the competing business first adopted its use of the disputed trademark (Did they adopt and start using the trademark before you?)**

- **Whether or not you have received notice that customers or potential customers are confused**

- **Whether or not the trademark used by the competing business is identical or confusingly similar to your trademark**

## What does TM mean?

When used within or near a word, design, or phrase, TM stands for "trademark" and indicates that the person or entity publishing the name is claiming certain rights to that name. These rights generally indicate what are deemed common-law rights, which are usually limited and unenforceable. Many companies will use TM prior to obtaining registration.

## What does ® mean?

The ® symbol when used within or near a word, design, or phrase stands for "registered" and indicates that the word, design, or phrase has been registered with the USPTO. Unlike common-law rights, the ® symbol does have significant legal implications and provides notice to others that, because the word, design, or phrase is registered, any infringers would be subject to the penalties afforded by U.S. federal law, which include, among other things, triple damages.

## When should I start using the ® with my trademark?

It is recommended (but not mandatory) that you begin using the ® symbol immediately after you receive registration with the USPTO. It is not necessary that you discard your old materials with the TM symbol, but you should modify the materials to use the ® at the next opportunity.

## Should I use the ® every time I write the word or display the registered design?

There are no formal guidelines as to how often you should use ® when writing in any particular document. It is recommended that you utilize ® for any prominent use (such as headers on advertising copy or a web page). If you are utilizing the word, design, or phrase on something that does not have a prominent display of it, then utilize the ® at the first use of the trademark in the document. It is not necessary or recommended to insert ® at every use. You should use ® for anything permanent such as interior or exterior signage or billboard displays.

CHAPTER 13

# FIT IN OR
# STAND OUT

CamachosCleaning.com
503-569-4974

Camacho's
CLEANING

HOUSEKEEPING • NEW CONSTRUCTION

# Where do you go from here?

If you already have a brand, I hope this book has helped you to become a student of branding and to be introspective about your current brand. Ask yourself if it's really serving its purpose and living up to its potential. Chances are very high that it's not. We've covered the reasons why your brand may not be working, whether it's poor naming, amateur logos, and everything in between. What sets apart the most successful companies is what they choose to do about it.

There are lots of owner egos wrapped up in their brand. I get it. You're proud of it. But is your ego going to be the thing that holds you back from making your business even more successful?

That's your call, of course. As I've said, you don't know what you don't know. For all those who won't change, there are plenty who are investing in their branding. Those companies are spending less on their marketing. They're building a better culture. Their recruitment is easier.

But the market will always predominantly be littered with more poorly branded companies than well-branded ones. And as I've said many times in this book, that means one thing: *opportunity*. It will never be less expensive to rebrand than it is right at this very moment. Your cost to implement a rebrand continues to rise the longer you wait. And it's not just the hard costs for re-wrapping trucks, changing uniforms and websites, and so on; it's the cost of lost sales opportunities and not becoming top-of-mind to your customers. It's the cost of building a better culture for your workforce and attracting and retaining your top employees. And of course, it's the lost dollars being earned by better-branded companies when you decide to exit your business.

**At the end of the day, you really have two choices: to fit in or to stand out. To bland or to brand. Choose wisely.**

Made in the USA
Las Vegas, NV
15 September 2024